FROM PHELPS TO GIELGUD

SARAH BERNHARDT

FROM PHELPS TO GIELGUD

REMINISCENCES OF THE STAGE THROUGH SIXTY-FIVE YEARS

BY

SIR GEORGE ARTHUR

With an introduction
by
JOHN GIELGUD

Essay Index Reprint Series

BOOKS FOR LIBRARIES PRESS
FREEPORT, NEW YORK

First published 1936
Reprinted 1967

INTERNATIONAL STANDARD BOOK NUMBER:

0-8369-0160-6

LIBRARY OF CONGRESS CATALOG CARD NUMBER:

67-23174

PRINTED IN THE UNITED STATES OF AMERICA

AUTHOR'S NOTE

THIS volume, written under difficult conditions, would scarcely have been written at all but for the expert advice and substantial help of Mr. Gilbert Wakefield, to whom I would tender my sincere thanks.

All aware as I am of the unprofessional nature of the book, I yet dare to dedicate it to those friends behind the curtain who, week by week and year by year, add so largely to the sum of healthy human joys.

G. A.

INTRODUCTION

Dear Sir George,

I was always stagestruck, as you can imagine, and when I was a boy there were many stories I used to beg my father to tell me about the theatre. Your book has delighted me by recalling many like them, and I feel more surely than ever that good acting must be a splendid and delightful thing, if it can give so much pleasure in the recollection of it.

My father's heroines were many of them the same as yours. Modjeska, whom he knew quite well, as she was a country-woman of his; Ada Rehan, whose Rosalind he loved; Sarah of course. How well I remember his description of the crush at the Pit of the old Lyceum on first nights, and how he would fight his way in to a very hard seat to revel in the play, and stare at all the famous ones in the stalls and boxes, especially at Kate Terry and her daughters, one of whom interested him particularly.

All these stories of his are nearly as familiar to me as my own cherished recollections of the theatre, and when I talk of them to him and read of yours, so like them, in this book, I can almost believe I was there myself, sharing some of the wonderful evenings you and he must have spent watching the

9

great ones, and storing up lovely moments from their performances to delight you all through your life and delight us in the
telling of them. It is really something for actors to be proud
of, is it not, if they can give such lasting pleasure as this in
their unequal, ephemeral public lives ?

For my own part I shall never forget seeing Sarah once in
" Le Drapeau," just as you so well describe her ; Duse once
in " Ghosts," and Ellen Terry many times (but alas ! she
was old, too) dancing on to the stage in " The Merry Wives,"
sailing across it as Portia, and once, most wonderful of all,
a night when I heard her read Beatrice with a club of amateurs
in Grosvenor Square. Read it ! she threw away the book after
the first few lines and acted it gaily, vividly, just like a young
woman, till in the Church scene, behold her swimming through
a barricade of gilt chairs and enfolding Hero in her arms, to
that young lady's acute embarrassment. But these memories
and some others of my own particular favourites that I hope
I shall never forget—Meggie Albanesi in " A Bill of Divorce-
ment " saying " You'll give her my love ! "—Claire Eames
in " The Silver Cord "—Hawtrey in " Home and Beauty "
—forgive me, you'll be thinking I want to write my reminiscences
as well as this poor introduction to yours—all these are hardly
more vivid to my mind or dearer to my imagination than the
images I can conjure up from all I have read and heard of the
great ones of the last century.

Of course, the better great acting moments are described,
the more one longs to know every detail of the rest of the performance. To read Craig's minute description of Irving's

entrance in " The Bells," Agate on the death of Sarah in " La Dame aux Camellias," to know how they looked or spoke or moved, how they bowed before the curtains or drove away to supper afterwards, it is so tantalizing that one can never see the whole play, those particular actors, cannot judge whether one would have felt the same towards them if one had been there to see.

I have always been so stagestruck myself, to the exclusion of everything else, that I wondered for a moment if your book would be so fascinating to others unconnected with the theatre as it is to me. Fortunately you are a member of the audience yourself and (knowing what joy an audience can give us actors) I can only conclude that there are many like you to whom the theatre is a continual pastime and enthusiasm and who bring to the theatre, as you do, not the indiscriminate hysteria of the addict, not the overfed sufferance of the casual looker-in at " shows," but a courteous interest in the changes and chances of our profession, allied to a real appreciation of the quality of plays and their performance. To these your book cannot fail to be of absorbing interest and a wonderful record of a great epoch in the theatre. And every actor will love to read it, for from an actor's point of view you are the ideal playgoer.

Yours most sincerely,

JOHN GIELGUD.

New Theatre,
November 2nd, 1935.

CONTENTS

13

CONTENTS

ILLUSTRATIONS

CHAPTER I

BEFORE MY TIME

TO have watched with eager interest Tomaseo Salvini and John Gielgud in *Hamlet*, to have heard Jenny Lind sing in a drawing-room and Grace Moore at the Opera House, to have applauded Marie Wilton—as such —in Tom Robertson's cup-and-saucer comedies, and to have been one of an enthusiastic audience for Marie Tempest's Jubilee; to have seen Sam Phelps play Bottom incomparably and Jack Hawkins Oberon ideally, to know the ripeness of Mrs. Stirling's nurse and the richness of Edith Evans's, to remember Charles Warner as young Steerforth on the stage and to admire Hugh Williams in the same character on the screen, to be able to compare Sam Sothern's nonchalance in *Dundreary* with Mackenzie Ward's in *The Wind and The Rain*, to have been taken to *Babil and Bijou* at Covent Garden in 1870 and to *Glamorous Night* at Drury Lane in 1935—all this is not to claim any knowledge of the theatre, still less any capability to appraise or criticize anything that takes place within it. It is only a reminder that one drank at the fountain of dramatic art in early childhood and

17   B

that one continues to swallow the same stimulating draught long after second childhood may be thought to have set in.

Further to have tasted—when a simple soldier in the early '80's—of the hospitality of Giulia Ristori in Rome, of Sarah Bernhardt in Paris, of Henry Irving, Charles Wyndham, the Kendals, the Bancrofts, and Modjeska in London, and yet to be the recipient—in undistinguished old age—of countless kind acts and words from young artists of the day, suggests that Peg Woffington's dictum can be improved on and that " Beneath tinselled robes hearts can beat very warm as well as very true."

Irresistible then has been the temptation to try and set out, without falling into the snare of reminiscence, a few of the contributions which, in three generations, the Stage has made to the enjoyment of humanity in general and of London in particular.

To point to any date, or any event, and pronounce it as the beginning of a new era is to ensure contradiction from " someone who knows better." It is a commonplace to assert that the dawn of the drama as we know and appreciate it to-day is to be dated back just seventy years, and to be credited to the production by the Bancrofts of Tom Robertson's *Society*. The occasion marked a chapter, and a most important chapter, in the story of the English theatre, and it would be ungracious and grossly unfair to belittle it in any degree. Even if he had no other claim—and he has many—to be remembered for honour, Tom Robertson would always stand as the first stage director imbued with the notion that a play, like a plant, should be carefully cultivated and trimmed before it is exhibited. He insisted—and apparently he was the first to do so—that later rehearsals should embrace the effects till then usually kept secret up to the first performance ; it was a system which had caused actors, knowingly or unknowingly, to disconcert one another and destroy an author's motif by the introduction of " bits of business " often entirely out of keeping with the demands of the play or the requirements of the character. W. S. Gilbert, in these matters more apt to be a tutor than a pupil, wrote handsomely :

" I frequently attended Robertson's rehearsals and learnt a great deal from his methods, which were quite a novelty. I look upon stage management as now understood as having been absolutely invented by him."

If Tom Robertson did not actually set in motion, he anyhow gave vigorous impulse to the tendency towards the realistic drama we enjoy to-day, but the tendency itself is of much earlier growth. Shakespeare's ideal of realism as interpreted by Hamlet to the Players may be but distantly related to what is understood by the term at this moment, but from that day until now it is

Circumstance which has largely prescribed theatrical methods and theatrical means.

Elizabethan plays were acted, and continued to be so acted for over a century, in the midst of the audience. There was no separated stage as we know it. There was no curtain, and " Enter So-and-So " and " Exeunt Omnes " at the beginning and end of each scene were indispensable directions. There was, of course, no scenery ; the necessary properties were carried on to the stage in full view of the audience. Above all, there was no picture-frame to set off the play as something actually happening—seen, as it were, through a transparent wall. In a word, there was no attempt to create that illusion of reality which is now the very essence of theatrical production.

The actors played not only in the midst of the spectators, but to and at them. Thus a tradition of rhetorical declamatory acting was set afoot which was carried on long after the stage was separated from the auditorium. A protruding platform, or proscenium, was to survive like a useless and dangerous appendix, and from the proscenium rather than the scene behind it the actors strove to stir the emotions of the audience. With this traditional method of acting burnt into their minds the playwrights penned their comedies, farces and dramas ; small wonder that the birthday of what we in 1935 understand by " realism " was still two and a half centuries ahead when William Shakespeare, with Hamlet as his mouthpiece, gave his priceless advice to the intelligent Vagabonds.

Wycherley and Congreve, and *a fortiori* Sheridan and Goldsmith, stepped forward towards realistic drama, nor did the process halt during that barren epoch (from the point of view of drama as distinct from acting), the first sixty years of the nineteenth century. But the move was in very slow time largely because the monopoly of legitimate play production was confined to two vast theatres where only classical, or quasi-classical, plays were suitable to the conditions. The smaller theatres then springing up and competing for popularity were restricted until nearly half-way through the century to what might be called the side-line goods of theatrical entertainment. The origin of the monopolies had a fine ironical flavour. Charles II had only sat on the throne for two years when he granted exclusive " patents " to Killigrew and Davenant, both personal friends ; they, and they only, had the right of running a theatre. There may have been sound social reasons to support the Royal decree ; the rival theatres were quite probably what officialdom would now call " of an undesirable character." Still, on the lips of the monarch in whose reign and with whose favour the " legitimate " English drama was to be more bawdy and amoral than at any other period in history, this Proclamation seems superbly hypocritical :

" Whereas We are given to understand that certain

persons . . . do frequently assemble for the performing and acting of Plays . . . which said Plays, as We are informed, do contain much matter of prophanation and scurrility, so that such kinds of entertainment, which, if well managed, might serve as Morall instructions in humane life, as the same are now used do for the most part tend to the debauching of the manners of such as are present at them, and are very scandalous and offensive to all pious and well-disposed persons."

" Patent theatres " were thus launched on a course of official monopoly that was to last for about a couple of centuries. But when legislation is in sharp conflict with public opinion, a way round the law is generally discovered and exploited. So, in unblushing defiance of the law, minor theatres sprang up, flourished and for seventy-five years flouted the monopolists with impunity. The Patent theatres appealed to the Courts, but the magistrates declined to interpret the law in their favour, and monopoly would probably have been wiped out had not some of the " minor " theatres made use of the drama for political satire of amazing virulence and daring. Fielding finally overstepped the mark. In his attacks on Authority—in plays which he wrote and produced when managing the old Haymarket Theatre—he provoked Walpole to counter-attack with the Licensing Act of 1737. This not only established our present Censorship, but confined the production of plays to the two great Patent theatres of Drury Lane and Covent Garden. The old monopolies then dug themselves in again for another hundred years and progress might have been arrested altogether had not Garrick instituted two important reforms when manager of Drury Lane in 1746. It was to him intolerable that the stage should be encumbered with spectators who often deliberately interfered with the performance and anyhow by their very presence on the scene precluded any effect of reality. Worse, on " Benefit Nights," in order to swell the takings, a sort of grandstand was erected at the back of the stage to hold additional lookers-on. David Garrick boldly swept the audience from the stage, leaving it free for the actors and the play, and almost with the same " motion " introduced footlights to reinforce the very feeble illumination of the chandeliers. Here was surely a long step forward towards our modern picture stage and its mirror of life.

Garrick was a no less benevolent revolutionary as regards acting. " If this young man is right," rather peevishly said his rival Quin, " then we are all wrong." Garrick was certainly " right " in recognizing that the duty of an actor is to listen no less than to talk.

" When three or four are on the stage with him, he is attentive to all that is spoke and never drops his character when he has finished a speech, *by either looking contemptuously on an inferior performer, unnecessary spitting, or suffering his eyes to wander through the whole circle of spectators.*"

One contrasts this pleasant habit in vogue among Garrick's predecessors with Lucien Guitry allowing the

23

curtain to rise while he was in the middle of a speech and thus giving the audience the feeling that they had actually interrupted a conversation.

Such was Garrick's success that Quin retired in a huff to Bath. But the " retirements " of artists are often little more than temporary and it was not long before Quin wanted to return, although he would not say so in so many words. " I am at Bath. Yours, James Quin," he wrote to the manager of Covent Garden. " Stay there and be damned. Yours, John Rich," was the terse reply he received.

Garrick's reforms did not include the question of costume, and he seemed to have no scruple about appearing in plays, whatever their period, in everyday eighteenth-century clothes, the audiences being of course blissfully unconscious of any absurdity or even of any anachronism.

There was a fair trial of how little costume really matters if the play is familiar when *Hamlet* was done in everyday dress a few years ago. The anachronism was so obvious that the audience was at first disposed to laughter, but the play soon dominated them so far that the absurdity of Hamlet in " modern dress " was forgotten. It was even said by some intelligent folk that the true position of Hamlet was for the first time made clear. In costume and impersonated by a stalwart star actor, with Claudius and Gertrude often played by artists of little value, Hamlet appears so obviously the most important person at the Court of Denmark that one does not quite understand why he does not make short work of his usurping uncle. But when the Prince was played by an unknown youth in an ill-fitting dinner-jacket, Claudius and Polonius in their grown-up tail coats and white waistcoats being manifestly his elders and betters, one appreciated for the first time how impossibly big his task of vengeance must have seemed to him.

Indisputably, Garrick drew crowds to Drury Lane by sheer acting ; the player and not the play was the attraction. His storm of rhetoric would have swept the audience from their seats had not the electric shock he imparted held them down. That he declaimed his speeches *à la mode* of the day is certain, yet France and Italy, which he toured with unqualified success, were forward to applaud him for identifying himself with every character he took on.

After Garrick's retirement in 1776 the next star at Drury Lane was Mrs. Siddons. She had actually appeared there in Garricks' time but was then so incapacitated by nervousness that she had been a " flop " and withdrew to the provinces to gain experience and confidence. She returned to the Lane with her brother, the famed Kemble, there to score many triumphs. But this so-called " great " period was of purely histrionic importance and contributed little but " history " to the English drama ; Mrs. Siddons and her brother excelled greatly, but they excelled on traditional lines, and it remained for Edmund Kean to break away from them. When, after a single rehearsal, he made his début as Shylock at Drury Lane, he startled everybody, and his manager in particular, by his lapse from orthodoxy. " Sir," cried the excited functionary, " this will never do ! It is quite an innovation ! It cannot be permitted ! " The answer was conclusive. " Sir, I wish it to be so," and " so " it continued to be whenever Kean took the stage.

Byron saw " life, nature, truth, without exaggeration or diminution " in Kean's *Richard III*. One wonders what we should see could we watch him with unprejudiced eyes to-day. One wonders how much of an art so delicate as Kean's was lost in the vastness of old Drury Lane, and then one remembers that when Wilton was cast to play with Kean in *The Merchant of Venice*, the great actor said " We must rehearse together, otherwise you will be too much startled this evening." The rehearsal was thorough, but when the evening came, Wilton was admittedly so terrified by Kean's stupendous violence that he very nearly lost his head and fled from the stage.

After Edmund Kean another pioneer, William Macready. Well-born, a scholar, an artist, a devotee of Shakespeare, and incidentally the father [1] of the

[1] That so distinguished, and so scientific, a soldier as Sir Nevile Macready should be thus sired was a matter which considerably excited the French Generals in the war. " C'est épatant, c'est le fils d'un acteur " was the sort of comment which fell, not infrequently, from the lips of our allies regarding the Adjutant-General of the British Expeditionary Force.

26

Adjutant-General of the British Army in the Great War, he was, according to Augustin Filon, the French critic, "the first to see the coming of realism." Macready was forward, if not foremost, to try, while retaining all the poetry of the lines, to bring out by the use of intelligent emphasis, their full meaning. No more of the "sound and fury signifying nothing" mode of acting. In short, yet another step towards realism.

But just now things, as well as the man, were contributing to this desired end. The public was deserting Drury Lane and Covent Garden ; the two great Patent theatres were dying a natural death, but dying in poverty and something like squalor. One manager of Drury Lane, when trying to run it for a couple of years, was said to have lost £50,000, a staggering sum in those days, however easy it might be to recoup to-day. In 1832 a Select Committee was appointed by the House of Commons to probe the whole question of the theatre ; they reported against the monopolies, but a Bill, based on their recommendations, was barely defeated in the House of Lords. One last attempt was made to save the "legitimate" theatres ; Macready was appointed manager of Covent Garden and men like Browning and Leigh Hunt were set to write plays for him. "Write me a drama and save me from going to America," Macready begged of young Browning to little effect ; the last effort to preserve the monopolies had its only fruit, pretty good fruit, in Bulwer's *Lady of Lyons*, and in the early '40's, under the Theatre Regulation Act, the present system of free trade was established. The public were manifestly pleased ; they had had enough of the old close order and were looking for entertainment in other, and more liberal, quarters. Chief among these new distractions was the Opera ; Society was flocking to the King's Theatre in the Haymarket, the home of grand opera and ballet, just as fifty years later, with Melba and the De Reszkes as the attraction, they flocked, under august ægis, to Covent Garden ; it was rather " the thing " for smart young people to affect ignorance of where Drury Lane and Covent Garden were located, but to be greatly hurt if anyone suggested they had not been to the Italian Opera.

But apart from the Opera, London at this time had several comparatively new and smaller theatres which were drawing playgoers away from the old out-moded Patent houses. They had had to be run on unorthodox lines till the law of 1843, and many were the ingenious devices used to evade the prohibitions of the law. At the Strand, for instance, the money for admission was taken through a window, to avoid prosecution for illegally taking money " at the doors." The whole history of these so-called " minor " theatres, and of the long and strenuous fight they put up, can be found—and indeed is very well worth finding—in Watson Nicholson's " The Struggle for a Free Stage in London " ; their origin is traced to a tavern in High Street, Marylebone Gardens, which, at one time the resort of men of fashion, had later fallen into disrepute, and had been the scene of Macheath's debaucheries in *The Beggar's Opera*. About 1740, however, these Gardens were reopened for evening concerts, with firework exhibitions ; these concerts merged eventually into that troublesome, because ambiguous, form of entertainment, the " burletta." By the end of the century the term was familiar, and signified " a drama in rhyme, entirely musical, consisting of recitative and singing, wholly accompanied, more or less, by the orchestra." As such, the burletta was a legal form of entertainment, not competing with the " legitimate drama " of the Patent theatres. But the term was subsequently extended to cover a performance of *Macbeth*, transformed into a ballet with music (1809), and in 1830 it was alleged in the House of Commons that *Othello* had been performed as a burletta, a triumph of ingenuity " accomplished by having a low pianoforte accompaniment, the musician striking a chord once in five minutes, and always so as to be totally inaudible " ! Such were some of the contrivances of the little theatres to defeat the monopoly.

But the Patent theatres were also at one time, and very ironically, injured by their very privilege. The law in 1831 was that these two theatres had to be closed on the Wednesdays and Fridays during Lent ; and the then Lord Chamberlain (the Duke of Devonshire) flatly declined to allow a performance of *Moses in Egypt* at

Drury Lane ; while at Covent Garden, as the " London Times " ironically phrased it :

" a sacred drama, on the story of Jephtha, conveying solemn impressions, from some of Handel's finest music, is prohibited as a profanation of this period of fasting and mortification."

Yet the " minor " theatres, not being under the Lord Chamberlain's high authority, could continue uninterruptedly throughout Lent to give what the manager of Drury Lane described bitterly as " a variety of entertainments of a mixed and ribald character," including *inter alia* an actress in " The Delineation of the Passions," the singing of negro melodies, a troupe of Bedouin Arabs, " Imitations of London Actors," and an entertainment called " A Wallet of Whims and Waggeries."

Paradoxical as this situation undoubtedly was, it has its almost exact parallel to-day, for though the law enforces Sunday closing on the theatres, we have an unlimited supply of other entertainments " of a mixed and ribald character." The plays of Shakespeare are too secular apparently for Sunday ; not even *The Miracle* with its Madonna is allowed to desecrate our English so-called Sabbath. But, thanks to the Sunday Performances (Regulation) Act of 1931, on every Sunday evening and in countless cinemas throughout the country, the British public is allowed to see such edifying spectacles as gangster-films and films about what are euphemistically called gold-diggers. Every Sunday you can visit Chambers of, no doubt educative, Horrors and see murderers in waxen effigy. Again, if your taste should lie in that direction, there are non-stop vaudeville entertainments to delight you. Or, supposing these are too old-fashioned for you, there is nothing to prevent sadists sitting in suburban music-halls to watch stalwart, semi-nude men miming the agonies of all-in wrestling. In brief, there is hardly any form of " questionable " entertainment that you cannot pay to see on Sundays. But you cannot see a play !

The chief contribution of the minor theatres was that they served to scotch the Patent tyrants and abolish the outrageous monopolies of Drury Lane and Covent Garden ; and as the law forbade them to present the old traditional drama, they had to devise and concoct new forms of non-legitimate entertainment. Their earliest experiments were confined to burlesques, lurid melo-dramas and trivial farces ; this was inevitable, as the upstarts must cater for those folk who had no appetite for the solid fare offered by the " established " theatres, for who might be termed the low-brow playgoers of the day. There was a good deal of shaking of heads and shrugging of shoulders. What would be the fate of the Drama, it was asked, now that every theatre, in *esse* and *posse*, had a free hand to compete in pleasing the public, and

perhaps placing very unwholesome titbits before them ?
" The Athenæum " was moved to mournful periods, and
the " Theatrical Times " agreed with a melancholy corre-
spondent who wrote : " Never perhaps in the recollection of the oldest playgoers have dramatic prospects
appeared more gloomy and discouraging." " The
Times " itself complained that " a certain elevated class
of the people, by shunning English theatres, might soon
lose sight of the native drama altogether." But at this
juncture a helping hand was stretched out from a high
quarter. The bright idea occurred to one of the Royal
entourage that variety might be given to the rather
ponderous Christmas festivities at Windsor by the introduction of " theatricals." The Queen and Prince Consort
caught at the idea : they reminded each other how greatly
they had enjoyed the recitations which Rachel had given
before them at Buckingham Palace, and they sent for
Charles Kean and asked him if he would be so good as to
" direct " (the word has come into vogue again) dramatic
performances at Windsor, the Rubens room in the Castle
to serve as a theatre. The reproductions were to be of the
best quality, no trouble was to be spared, artists of first
water were to be engaged, and in Christmas week of 1848
the Keans and Keeleys led off with *The Merchant of Venice*.
From then until the death of the Prince Consort—
except when the demise of the Queen Dowager and the
stress of the Crimean War forbade any rejoicings—
" theatricals " were an annual institution ; in a dozen of

32

Shakespeare's plays, and twice that number of lighter pieces, such names as Macready,[1] Phelps, Charles Mathews, Ben Webster and Buckstone figured on sumptuous programmes, and Victoria not only permitted but led the applause which, without her consent, would have been a breach of etiquette. " The Times " took heart and hoped that the Windsor theatricals might issue in " a new stock of dramatists." But the hope was doomed to disappointment ; no English dramatic author imposed himself on public attention, and the public were querulously accused of having " vitiated taste " and of only caring for the " light and frivolous emanations of French writers."

The advantages which the " light and frivolous emanations " offered to impresarios was their cheapness —translations were quickly, and roughly, done and poorly paid for. Tom Taylour only received £150 for the melodrama which proved a blazing success, *The Ticket-of-Leave Man*, because it was reckoned as an adaptation. Tom Robertson himself (oh the pity of it !) occupied some of life's best hours in re-adapting for East End audiences West End " adaptations from the French," many of which had been due to the deftness of dramatic critics who thought to swim with the tide. It seemed for awhile as if the tide were ebbing altogether ; playwrights

[1] So great was the Queen's admiration for Macready that when he took farewell of the stage in February 1851 she insisted, though at some personal inconvenience, on attending the occasion.

of merit were nowhere to be found, productions were cheap and sometimes nasty, and the entire absence of young aspirants to theatrical fame moved Clement Scott, then himself just moving towards the front as a dramatic critic, to write scornfully of " old fossils who persisted in playing young lovers and dashing sparks when they were rapidly qualifying for the rôle of Grandfather." The Crimean campaign, the Indian Mutiny, the fear (in 1859) of universal war, the death of the Prince Consort and consequent long mourning were responsible for a long stretch of social depression with which the theatre sadly synchronized. Then there was a sudden rift in the clouds and the happy not only happened but remained. The Bancrofts arrived and " took over " theatrical management ; Tom Robertson struck hands with them in theatrical authorship. The combination came into being just seventy years ago and, however little importance was attached to it, it proved to be the saving health of the British Drama.

CHAPTER II

THE BANCROFTS

THE theatre was in this rather sorry and shoddy condition when, just seventy years ago, a young couple then engaged to be married—the fiancée some seven years the elder of the two—started in management with a (borrowed) thousand pounds in the bank, the lease of a theatre in a Bloomsbury slum at a weekly rental of £20 in their pockets, and a rooted determination to brighten things up. Sydney Bancroft, as Sir Squire Bancroft was then known, had started his career by playing with Madame Celeste in the *Green Bushes* and had then in truth gone through the mill, having, for instance, been called upon to study and play Cassio, Gratiano, and three other, and even longer, parts within a fortnight. Marie Wilton was already a popular London favourite and, with the solitary exception of Nellie Farren, surely no " principal boy " in burlesque ever took so many hearts by storm. The joint manager, a position to which matrimony was soon to entitle him, had a shrewd and sound business head, the manageress had a special flair for choosing the right pieces irrespective as to whether or no she and her husband played the lead. Within a little more than three years the £1,000, which had melted into £125 before the curtain rose on the first night, had long been repaid, the tumbledown " Queen's " had been converted into a cosy and charmingly decorated theatre to which the Heir Apparent willingly lent his name and to which fashionable folk flocked, although their coachmen had some difficulty in finding it. Meanwhile Marie Wilton—who had put herself in the salary list at £10 a week—had bidden good-bye both to burlesque and to H. J. Byron, and Tom Robertson, who when he joined forces with this delightful couple was in such low financial water that he spoke of living on his pipe, had scored five signal successes, most of them capable of repeated revival, in *Society*, *Ours*, *Caste*, *M.P.* and more especially *School*. There are still a few to remember how the two-hundred-and-fiftieth performance of *School* took place in a fog which increased in density as the evening wore on, and the then Prince and Princess of Wales had to be escorted back to Marlborough House by a posse of torch-bearing police.

Bancroft had a definite policy in mind. He was determined—and his wife no less so—to make, within his means, the theatre, or anyhow their own theatre, a mirror of real life ; his plays should be carefully, and even elaborately dressed, with every detail thoroughly thought out and put into effect. All that he had in view ran clean contrary to all he had known in the past. He had been

LADY BANCROFT

[Facing p. 36

told by an old manager, who thought he knew his job,
that small talk would never draw paying audiences ;
what these wanted was declamation or broad farce, or else
plenty of blue fire and mysterious disappearances. The
Bancrofts set out to specialize in small talk, but the talk
must be good and the artists in whose mouths it was put
must be carefully selected and their services as far as
possible retained. Loyal and intelligent team work, not
merely the ragged result of a stock company, was their
object, in pursuit of which they never swerved. To Bancroft came the idea of making a single play form the
entire programme, a thing hitherto unknown when even
the pantomime, beginning at seven o'clock, was preceded
by a farce or, so-called, operetta. There was moreover
in mind the memory of Macready struggling to amass
sufficient money to secure before retirement a thousand a
year with which to bring up his family ; salaries at the
Prince of Wales's, however modest, should be worthy of
the name and not a mere pittance such as the £2 a week
which John Hare, one of the earliest recruits to the Prince
of Wales's company, had till then received.

If the soldier is to fight well he must be fed well ; if
he is to make himself efficient, he must—as far as conditions allow—be made comfortable ; if he is to respect
himself in his profession he must be adequately remunerated ; if he is to give of his best to his country his
country must do its best for him. Such was the axiom
of the greatest military organizer of the last half-century,

and it may well be that in his organization of a theatre
Bancroft had in mind the same blend of philanthropy and
practical politics. He saw—it is difficult to conjecture
why no one else saw it—that, apart from the acting itself,
the whole theatrical system cried for reform, and the first
which he instituted did a very great deal to secure
approval of what was to follow. He found, to his surprise, that the arrangements for paying weekly salaries
under which, as a struggling young actor, he had writhed
in the provinces, held good in London. Every Saturday
morning actors and actresses, whatever their standing,
would join up with carpenters, cleaners, and dressers
outside the treasury to receive their weekly remuneration ;
Bancroft's was the reform under which an emissary from
the department tapped at the artists' doors and handed in
the cheque or cash for services rendered.

Reforms, he was sure, must be partnered by innova-
tions.

Matinées are now so "taken for granted" as an
institution that one is a little dismayed to remember
oneself the time when the pantomime enjoyed a monopoly
of them. The Bancrofts in 1869 put on an afternoon
performance of *School*, then at the height of its success,
but the experiment, in familiar phrase, did not "come
off" and was only repeated some six years later to enable
Sothern to see Mrs. Bancroft in *Sweethearts* ; then to make
up the programme for a morning performance Ellen
Terry played with the actor-manager in Gilbert's very

slight comedietta, *The Happy Pair*. This time the notion caught on and *Peril*—adapted from Sardou's *Nos Intimes*—was frequently, if fitfully, given in the afternoon. But with *Diplomacy* matinées were regularly established—on Wednesdays and Saturdays—although for some time they required separate announcements and advertisements. The originators justly insisted on paying full, i.e. extra, salaries not only to the performers but to the whole staff of the theatre on whom, as they said, the equivalent of a night's labour was imposed.

Sixty years ago the price of the stall was raised from 7s. to 10s., or 10s. 6d., a figure at which it may almost be said to be stabilized with, of course, the modern imposition of a tax. The reason for the rise can be traced to the impossibility of running *The School for Scandal*, with its costly production and comparatively costly cast, at a small theatre at existing rates. The first to follow the example set by the "Prince of Wales's" was the "Gaiety"; the "Lyceum" was quickly on its heels, and before long 10s. 6d., at first with programme thrown in, was the order of the day. The expensive Cochran shows apart, it may sometimes to the casual observer seem a little unfair that for a play on which it costs, say, £500 to raise the curtain nightly, no more payment is exacted than for a comedy with only one scene to set and less than half a dozen artists to remunerate. But at least this can be said : that in London, whether places be booked at the theatre itself or at the libraries, the price is absolutely fixed, whereas in Paris, given a greedy agent and a wealthy, and perhaps impatient, client, the price of seats may soar into the region of fantasy and suggest itself as an insult to common sense. A week before the production of *Diplomacy* in 1878 the representative of an important theatrical library offered to buy up every stall in the theatre for six months and drew from his pocket a cheque for something like eighteen thousand pounds to complete the bargain. To his amazement the offer was declined [1] ; the astute manager was not going to risk his popularity with the public, and this would certainly have been threatened if the library in question had made a corner in stalls and charged their own sweet price for them.

In a word, to increase, and sustain, the dignity of their profession was the *mot d'ordre* of the Bancrofts, and their management unquestionably constituted a new era in the development of the English stage, and revived—or rather created anew—interest in clever plays dealing with the existing period.

For fourteen years the Bancrofts throve at the old " Prince of Wales's " ; their nightly expenses never exceeded £70,[2] and despite the failure of an expensive *Merchant of Venice*, in which Ellen Terry was an entrancing Portia and that fine actor, Charles Coghlan, a disastrous

[1] Three years later Irving would not on the occasion of a first night assign any seats to libraries which had made a corner in stalls for the sensational début of Mrs. Langtry in *Ours* at the Haymarket Theatre.

[2] At the " Haymarket " these varied from £100 to £120.

Shylock, and one or two minor disappointments, they had made a net profit which came to the edge of six figures. They disbursed money freely but judiciously; they spent themselves in fine effort. The long hours devoted to the British Museum, to the British Embassy in Paris, to Venice, to Knole and other historic country places in order to secure that hackneyed word "atmosphere"—and a good deal that was more substantial besides—bore fruit in productions which smacked but little of the stage as it was then known. Lady Sneerwell's genuine high marqueterie chair, Lady Teazle's genuine black page, the Minuet introduced into Sheridan's masterpiece, which inspired Val Prinsep's brush, the exact reproduction for *Money* of a card-room in a well-known club, the faithful copies of famous pictures at the Garrick Club for the greenroom of old Covent Garden Theatre in *Peg Woffington*, and the elimination of the tag to which Charles Reade had so persistently clung, the P. & O. saloon for the *Overland Route*, the equally thought-out, if simpler, setting for the Robertson comedies—all these, and a hundred other details, were eye-openers to a public for some of whom the Crummles were scarcely exaggerated types.

Then on a May evening in 1879 they learnt that Lord Kilmorey, having made to themselves the first offer, had secured as tenants for his newly acquired St. James's Theatre, an all-powerful trio in the persons of the Kendals and John Hare. Bancroft sniffed a challenge;

before noon the next day he had secured the remainder ‹
John Clark's lease of the Haymarket Theatre at an annual
rent of less than £5,000 with a pledge to spend £10,000
(actually twice that amount was laid out) on remodelling
and partially rebuilding a very out-of-date structure.
The remodelling, if eventually highly profitable, had for
its first result an unholy uproar from former " pittites,"
who found themselves deprived of their usual terrain.
The raucous and shrill cries of these injured parties may
still linger in the ears of the few survivors of that " first
night," and it certainly required all Bancroft's suave tact
and powers of persuasion to still the malcontents and
enable the curtain to be raised, on a foggy January night
in 1880, for a revival of *Money*, a *cheval de bataille* which
could always be relied upon either to fill up a gap or in
anything like an emergency.

The translation from the Prince of Wales's to the Haymarket was matched by the Bancrofts' own migration
from Cavendish Square to Berkeley Square, a not unimportant move at a time when Oxford Street formed a
distinct social frontier. But the little Sunday dinners
were no less delightful ; Mrs. Bancroft's Sunday after-
noons became a magnet of attraction when the week-end
habit was still unknown, and in her cosy, if rather airless,
drawing-room many plans were discussed, many friendships formed, and many pleasant hours whiled away.
Increasing fame and swelling coffers did nothing to spoil,
and a good deal to enlarge, hospitality to which the

" Bogeys," as they were familiarly called, had always been given.

But the time was at hand when entertainments need not be limited to Sundays, for after twenty years in the saddle, a very astute couple decided that a sum approximating £200,000 was sufficient for their needs and elected to retire from management, though not necessarily from the stage.

The Prince and Princess of Wales fixed the evening for the farewell to an honourable régime, and as soon as the date—the 20th July 1885—was announced, the theatre could have been sold out three times over, although in order to make more room, rather exiguous chairs were substituted for the stalls, and other ingenious makeshifts adopted. A certain number of seats were reserved up to the last days for personal friends, and the writer remembers telegraphing from the Sudan, where he had been engaged on the abortive Gordon Relief Expedition, to obtain a place, and arriving on the eve of the occasion. The playbill furnished the names of every artist of note : Irving delivered an ode written by Clement Scott, Mrs. Bancroft raised herself to the summit of her art in her rendering of her favourite Peg, Bancroft delivered an oration which did not err on the side of levity, and Mr. Alfred de Rothschild wound up the evening with a supper such as no other chef than his could compose.

The Bancrofts' appearances under other managements were very few. Mrs. Bancroft played Lady Franklin, as she alone could play it, in Hare's revival of *Money*, and rather over-elaborated a minor part in *Fédora* at the Haymarket—where she spoke of Tree's graceful courtesy to "one of his company," but complained that Mrs. Patrick Campbell was a little lacking in consideration in causing so long a wait before the last act as to endanger the comedy scene which she had written up for herself. Bancroft was tempted by Irving to play the Abbé Latour in *The Dead Heart* at £100 a week ; he handed over the whole amount to the Salvation Army, partly out of philanthropy, partly because he did not want his banker to think that his regular income was suddenly increased. The fencing scene between the two more than middle-aged and rather short-sighted men was a really fine exhibition and reminds one that the young actors of to-day might do well to practise a little more with the foils and fit themselves for the final scene in *Hamlet*. But just as Terriss had to say to Irving in the *Corsican Brothers* : "I say, Guv'nor, don't you think a few rays from the moon might fall on me," so Mrs. Bancroft gently remonstrated with her old friend that, owing to the disposition of the limelight in the "duel to the death," she could only see her husband's legs.

And last of all, in aid of a Children's Hospital in which Queen Mary has always taken special interest, there was given, with the Bancrofts' co-operation in their old parts, the "drum and trumpet" third act of *Ours*. The cast was made up entirely of managers and ex-managers down to the smallest parts, and although charity clothes very many shortcomings, it must be confessed that in many respects a more ragged performance has seldom been put on the regular stage.

CHAPTER III

ROME VAINCUE AND DIPLOMACY

IN 1876 the writer was sent to Paris to fill in a few of the many gaps left by an Eton education. Hard study was prescribed, but the theatre was permitted as part of the curriculum, and the Vaudeville, the Gymnase, the Odéon, the Porte St. Martin, and even the Palais Royal were on the programme. Jeanne Granier, still among us, was in the early down of her triumphant youth ; Rejane had not arrived ; beautiful Jane Harding was still in her childhood ; Pasca and Fargeuil stood for all that is meant by elegance and distinction, Celine Chaumont was at her merriest, but burnt into memory is the first visit to the Théâtre Français where Sarah Bernhardt was playing in *Rome Vaincue*.

The subject of the play was the guilty love and consequent punishment of a vestal virgin who had broken her vow of chastity. Sarah asked that this character might be enacted by the beautiful Mademoiselle Dudlay, she herself preferring to represent Posthumia, the girl's grandmother, an aged blind woman. The choice of what, at first sight, might have seemed the part of a crouching, croaking old beldame was curious, but was justified to the hilt. The facial make-up was marvellous, and the sides of the great cloak, which fell away when her arms were extended, suggested the wings of a huge and sinister bat. In the last act, the vestal virgin has been condemned to be buried alive with one loaf of bread and a jug of water to prolong the agony of starvation. To save her from the horrible torture, the grandmother hands her a knife with which to stab herself. The victim's hands are tied. The old woman unloosens the girl's white robe, and runs her fingers over the bare breast to find the spot beneath which lies the heart. " *C'est bien là ton cœur. Mon enfant, mon enfant !* " and the dagger is plunged home. The audience on the first night was as if electrified, and to those who, like the present writer, saw the play, although nearly half a century has elapsed, Sarah's whispers, Sarah's gestures, and Sarah's hoarse cry in this grim episode must be burnt into memory. In the final scene the corpse of the girl has been laid in a large and lonely tomb ; the stage is empty except for the old woman, who rises from where she is crouching in the corner, slowly and silently feels her way to the tomb, climbs the steps which lead up to it, beats gently on the door, and then again, the whisper which could be heard right across the house : " *Opimie, ma fille, ne me laisse pas seule. Ouvre donc, Opimie c'est ton aieule,*" and Sarah seemed to disappear into the shadow of the grave as the curtain came slowly down. The play

was a little heavy in the earlier parts, and proved only a
succès d'estime, although Sarah herself revived it for a
special function twenty years later ; its author attributed
all the success *Rome Vaincue* enjoyed to the interpretation
of the actress which exceeded in subtlety and power anything he had anticipated or conceived.

While Sarah was startling Paris with a new revelation
of her matchless gifts, Blanche Pierson was drawing
crowded houses at the Vaudeville to see her in Daudet's
Froment Jeune et Riesler Ainé, a play which suffered pretty
badly in adaptation for London. *Partners*, despite the
flavour which Tree's acting imparted to it, bore much
the same relation to the French original as a tinned
peach does to the ripe fruit gathered on a sunny afternoon from an old garden wall. Just then Victorien
Sardou was penning a new play, which was to prove one
of his best winners and to have a lease of life the expira-
tion of which is wholly problematical ; for Dora, the
title part, there could be no other choice than Pierson,
but it required a brain-wave to cast for the adventuress
Mademoiselle Bartet, whose representation of a little
blind work-girl in Daudet's drama might have drawn
tears from a stone.

The success of *Dora* was immediate and undoubted,
and Bancroft, who was revelling in the returns he was

enjoying from *Peril*, the English version of Sardou's *Nos Intimes*, took advantage of the enforced closing of his theatre on Ash Wednesday, hurried across the Channel, saw the play, saw himself in the three-men scene, wrote a cheque for £1,500—the largest sum till then ever paid for a foreign work, and handed the script to Clement Scott, with injunctions to keep as closely as possible to the lines of the original. One useful alteration was enjoined : Henry Beauclerc, instead of being a sailor friend, was to be converted into a diplomatist, and to be the much older brother of Julian.

Diplomacy—the title was only chosen after a dozen others had been set aside—has been described by experts as the most perfect example of Sardou's consummate skill in theatrical carpentry. Probably no play has been revived so often, and to such steady profit ; star casts have been always obtainable, while amateurs regard it with special favour, largely because it gives to the whole dramatis personæ almost an equal chance.

Yet although the level of acting has risen immeasurably since 1878, it is possible to think that the original cast at the old Prince of Wales's Theatre has never been equalled in excellence. John Clayton's ripe round method gave the correct impression that here was a brother, much older in years and experience than the young soldier, to whom he was tenderly devoted, and to whom he stood in *loco parentis*. Neither John Hare's fussiness nor Gerald Du Maurier's dryness, however

D

excellent their technique, conveyed the same notion. Then no one—with the possible exception of Ian Hunter —has ever given the sense of impetuosity and irresponsibility with which Kendal invested the attractive, but not very astute, Julian. It must be remembered that at that time the Military Attaché was not usually a—so to speak —scientific officer, but was selected rather for his breeding, appearance, and good manners. Miss Le Thière gave to the Marquise a sloppiness which made her hand-to-mouth existence the more explicable. Even Miss Gladys Cooper's flawless acting—how one wishes one could see Gladys Cooper play Zicka !— missed something of the pathos which Mrs. Kendal gave to such a line as " I have had so many of these offers that I have almost ceased to regard them as insults."

Curiously enough, the only weak points in the original production were to be found in the actor-manager himself and his wife. " Mrs. Kendal, peerless though her art is, could never play Fédora," said Bancroft to the present writer. " She is always the mother of British children." A tempting *tu quoque* would have been open to Mrs. Kendal. Squire Bancroft, admirable in many character parts, could only act inside the clothes, never inside the skin, of a Russian Count. Perhaps it is only fair to say that Orloff has only once been real on the English stage, and then as played by a Russian himself. Mrs. Bancroft was hopelessly miscast; an exquisite *comédienne*, whose laughter had always in it a suspicion of happy tears, was quite incapable of lending herself to any sinister plot, and Zicka has only once found a true representative in the person of Olga Nethersole.

Diplomacy was presented in January 1878, and Bancroft was not only *felix* in his company but in his opportunities. The Berlin Conference had not yet solved the Eastern question ; jingoism was on the lips of every Londoner, and while Mr. Gladstone's attitude rendered it difficult for a hostess to find anyone willing to meet him at dinner, the leading members of the Royal Family were said, at one moment, to be no less sharply split in their opinions than members of the Cabinet. Queen Victoria, leaning wholly on Lord Beaconsfield—whom she now regarded as the Oracle of Truth and the Ark of Salvation —and the Prince of Wales, quite justifiably irritated by the trend of events in Russia, were admittedly Turcophil, while the Princess of Wales and the Duke of Edinburgh were said to take their cue from Lord Derby and Lord Salisbury and affirm Russia's right to save Christian States from the clutches of the Infidel. The Queen sent a private message to the Tsar that in the event of a Russian advance on Constantinople British neutrality could not be guaranteed, while the Prince of Wales wrote scornfully about " sitting with hands folded " and " cutting a ridiculous figure in the eyes of the world."

So in 1877 England was on the brink of a war with

Russia, and the "secret plan" with its attendant sob-stuff was a much stronger stage proposition than it has ever been since. It is more than an open question whether the play would not always have gained by being put back to the hectic period when it was produced.

Two other details have always suggested themselves as glaring anachronisms. In the '70's and '80's men rode in the Bois, as in the Park, in the afternoon, and there would be nothing odd in Orloff making a call in correct riding-dress—cut-away coat, overalls, and spurs—at five o'clock; but to stride into a lady's drawing-room in breeches and butcher boots strikes a wrong note and is not "worth it" just for the sake of the unimportant business with the riding-switch.

And originally, when Henry Beauclerc detected the culprit through his olfactory sense, well-dressed women invariably wore long suede gloves, to which the perfume would cling and convey itself to any paper or letter. The bare hand which the modern Zicka always displays would be incapable of this, nor does it lend itself prettily to the business of a courtly diplomatist retaining it in his own and sniffing at it.

Even though the machinery of the drama may to-day creak and groan a little, *Diplomacy*, like Charity, never seems to fail, and Squire Bancroft's legacy to Gerald Du Maurier still has material, as well as theatrical, worth.

CHAPTER IV

SARAH IN LONDON, 1879

IN the summer of 1879 the Théâtre Français, for the first time for many a year, must close its doors for repairs, but its revenue must be kept up and the company must not be idle. The astute M. Perrin was meditating where and how to employ them when there came overtures from Mr. John Hollingshead, the impresario of the Gaiety Theatre, a genial soul who knew his business from A to Z, and who would move as easily and be as popular in the *coulisses* of a Court Theatre as in the saloon of a dancing-gaff at Wapping. M. Perrin boldly named his figure, which represented the average maximum of the Comédie, £1,000 a week, payable in advance. There was no haggling or hesitation. Hollingshead was out for a *coup*, closed with the terms, and it only remained to draw up the programme. This was ambitious enough as it included five of Molière's comedies, three of Racine's tragedies, Victor Hugo's *Hernani* and *Ruy Blas*, and at least a dozen other more modern pieces.

To the Directors of the Français the Sociétaires ranked

53

only by seniority, and Sarah's name came more than half-way down among the "mesdames." The list, a galaxy of talent, was headed by Madeleine Brohan, perhaps the greatest "grande dame" who ever trod the boards, and rounded off by Jeanne Samary, on whose delicious lines Miss Marie Tempest might be thought to have modelled herself. It was an all-star company, but the British public had already selected the star they wanted to gaze on, and from the moment that—rather sick and very sorry for herself—Sarah set foot on Folkestone Pier, she was the cynosure of every eye, and the favourite theme of every conversation, with special reference to duels lately fought by rival aspirants to her hand.

The English public followed her, mobbed her, applauded her, quoted her. At the great French bazaar in the Albert Hall even the Royal Personages present enjoyed an unusual immunity from over-pressing attention, so intense was the desire of the huge crowd to get a sight of—and possibly a word with—Sarah. People hung on every word she said in the theatre, they discussed everything she did—or was supposed to have done—outside it ; they surrendered themselves to a charm they could not define, to a personality they could not fathom, to a language with which many of them had but a bowing acquaintance.

Her first appearance was in the second act of *Phèdre* which formed part of the triple bill, and Sarah was perhaps never more a *traqueuse* than on this 4th of June. Ambitious young actors and actresses, whose heads are rightly hot and whose hands are rightly cold just before the rise of the curtain on a first night, take heart of grace by what happened to perhaps the greatest artist whom three generations have known. Three times she rouged her cheeks and blackened her eyelids, three times she sponged all off; she was sure she was too ugly; and she remembered she was too thin; she repeated to herself: " *Vers mon cœur tout mon sang se retire ; j'oublie en le voyant,*" and the word *oublier* reminded her that, brief though her scene would be, she was liable to forget her words. Finally, as she bent her head to receive the applause which greeted her appearance, she lost for one instant her artistic self-possession, and started on a note she had pitched too high, but had to retain through the whole scene. She suffered acutely, but then the very suffering made her acting the more intense. She wept real scorching tears.

She implored Hyppolite for the love which was consuming her, and the arms she stretched out to Mounet Sully writhed with sheer longing for his embrace. Her passion, which, with all its febrile force, never marred the purity of her diction, seemed to master—as it were—the last shred of her modesty, and when terrified at the effect that this guilty passion has provoked in Hyppolite, she strives to pull his sword from its sheath, and plunge it into her own breast, she swooned back in real and absolute collapse. The excitement of the audience was such as is seldom seen in a London theatre. Something quite unusual—quite beyond any experience or expectation—had occurred something which might never occur again. They had read of Rachel, now they had seen Sarah, and Sarah had set every nerve and fibre in their bodies throbbing, and had held them spellbound. They insisted on seeing the actress again, and would take no refusal, although they were told she had been carried to her dressing-room, and when the curtain at last rose in reply to their demand and disclosed Sarah, half held up by Mounet Sully, they gave her an ovation which she admitted never faded from her memory. She had come and suddenly conquered, and she was sure the London first night was definitive for her future. During the season she played in *Hernani, Zaire, Andromache, Ruy Blas, Le Sphinx,* and *Jean Marie* with unvarying success, and constantly deepening the impression she had made, but it is doubtful if any subsequent audience ever rose to the same fever temperature as Sarah's passion induced when she first met London across the footlights.

The six weeks spent in London provided a strange record of generous gestures and kindly actions, of engagements and excitements, of blazing triumphs and bitter attacks. Sarah was at once at her best and her worst ; she was exquisite but she was exasperating. She received hundreds of letters, many of which she never opened, few of which she ever answered ; she accepted invitations and at the last moment failed to appear, or disturbed all arrangements by preposterous unpunctuality. One happening gave something of an electric shock when the news of it reached Paris. Sarah was invited to dine at Marlborough House ; that this supreme social distinction should be conferred was of course the supreme tribute to her art, but it meant something more. It meant that Albert Edward and Alexandra, Prince and Princess of Wales—who enjoyed a virtual sovereignty over English Society and whose wishes and tastes a wide circle was eager to imitate—had determined that passports to their gracious hospitality should be offered to anyone claiming real or honourable distinction whether inherited or acquired. And certainly on this summer evening no guest was at once more perfectly dignified and more perfectly at ease than the woman who was to be entitled " reine d'attitudes " and " princesse des gestes." The Princess of Wales—as keen and constant a playgoer as the Prince—had seen Sarah in Paris the year before, during the great Exhibition, and had then determined she should be presented to her. For her part Sarah Bernhardt told the present writer that of all the illustrious personages with whom she came in contact—and they were many—one figure appealed to her perpetually and irresistibly ; she spoke of the Princess of Wales as of having at the time " blinded " her to everybody else present.

An instance of differential treatment thrusts itself into

recollection. The scene was a tea-party given in Paris by a Russian notability in honour of the Grand Duke and Grand Duchess Vladimir,[1] to which a group of *grandes dames*—few of them attended by their husbands—were invited. Madame Bartet, as a special favour, recited—as she alone could recite—some choice morsels of poetry. The already famous Sociétaire of the Comédie was not invited to stay to tea, and although all the men were solemnly presented to her, not one of the ladies, few of whom were models of conjugal fidelity, even said *bon jour* to an artist whose domestic life, moreover, compared very favourably with some of theirs. Shortly afterwards Madame Bartet came over to England for a series of performances, and to a friend who went to bid her good-bye at the station she explained that she had postponed her return to Paris for a day as she had been bidden by the Princess of Wales to come to tea at Marlborough House and meet the Queen of Denmark.

From the great English chorus which sang Sarah's praises in London there was one dissentient voice. Matthew Arnold had his doubts; but then Matthew Arnold could brook no rival to Rachel in his mind or memory. In his youth he had seen Rachel play *Hermione* at Edinburgh, had followed her to Paris, and for two

[1] Grandparents of the Duchess of Kent.

months never missed one of her representations. Such devotion has its recompenses ; it also has its prejudices and its penalties.

" Temperament," he wrote, " and quick intelligence, passion, nervous mobility, grace, smile, voice, charm, poetry—Mlle Sarah Bernhardt has them all. One watches her with pleasure, with admiration—and yet not without a secret disquietude. Something is wanting, or, at least, not present in sufficient force ; something which alone can secure and fix her administration of all the charming gifts which she has, can alone keep them fresh, keep them sincere, save them from perils by caprice, perils by mannerism. That something is high intellectual power. It was here that Rachel was so great ; she began, one says to oneself, as one recalls her image and dwells upon it—she began almost where Mlle Sarah Bernhardt ends."

Matthew Arnold, in comparing Rachel with Sarah, has of course most of his readers at a disadvantage, for few of them living within this century [1] could bear witness to

[1] General Sir George Higginson wrote to me under date of 1st June 1923 : " I first saw Rachel in Paris, when I was an Eton boy, and was passing my Easter holidays in 1841 with my people in that then rather dreary city. I can see Rachel now in the well-known scene in *Les Horaces*, where she denounces the Romans, ' Voir le dernier Roman a son dernier soupir moi seul en etre la cause et mourir de plaisir.' Nothing I have ever heard since made me shiver so with appreciation. I once heard her in comedy ; it was a failure. Her majestic figure and features could never relax into an attractive smile. I saw her some years later, probably in 1852 ; she had lost none of her power."

the talents of the former. In the veins of both flowed
the blood which distinguishes so many great artists.
Both shone with special lustre in the classic masterpieces.
Both glorified Racine and both attained their histrionic
zenith in *Phèdre*. Both also figured heroically in French
revolutionary and military crises. In justice to Rachel
it must be remembered that her brief career was always
a desperate race with Time, while Sarah had Time
altogether on her side, and before the mighty sum of her
total achievements, the record of Rachel cannot but
shrink.

The season in London added largely to Sarah's fame
and convinced her that her commercial value was almost
inestimable. Tempting offers to return here, dazzling
proposals to cross the Atlantic, attracted and aggravated
her; she could accept none of them, or anyhow turn none
of them to her own advantage. She was not the mistress
of her own life ; the Directors of the Français held her
fast bound ; she was determined to be set free from the
fetters, free to take her future into her own capable
hands and shape it without restraint or restriction.
She returned to Paris and rode for an artistic fall.

The opportunity soon arose. In March 1880, Emile
Augier's *L'Aventurière* was somewhat hurriedly put into

rehearsal and Sarah was bidden to study Dona Clorinde. She developed sore throat ; she was too unwell even to try on her costumes, she disliked the part, she thought the lines were bad poetry, and she told the author, with some heat, what she thought of his work. Rehearsals were too few and too hurried ; she asked for delay, and it was refused. On the evening of the 17th April, she was irritable because she played, as she admitted, badly ; looked, as she thought, ugly, and the next morning, while Mademoiselle Barretta was lauded to the skies, Sarah had a very bad Press—one writer going so far as to say that her gestures suggested Zola's Virginie rather than Augier's Clorinde. Sarah quivered with rage ; she had brought about her fall but it had hurt her more than she expected, and perhaps its bruises never entirely disappeared. Anger, though she would not admit it—when does an angry woman admit she is angry ?—guided her hand when without an hour's reflection she drafted her resignation to the Directors, sent copies of her letters to the *Figaro* and *Gaulois* and hurried from Paris so as to be free from advice and remonstrances which would surely descend on her.

At that time any secession from the Théâtre Français was an almost unheard-of event, and Sarah's rash act was resented, as much as regretted, by the Directors and the public alike. Whether or no she ever herself looked back wistfully to the Temple of Classic Drama where she had climbed to the topmost rung of the dramatic ladder, there is this anyhow to be said : that had she remained there, the public at large would have been a great loser. *Fédora*, *Théodora*, *La Tosca*, *La Sorcière*, *Gismonda*, *Thérèse* [1] might never have been called into being ; Cleopatra and Elizabeth would not have died for us ; Jeanne d'Arc's *La France re-naitra* would not vibrate in our ears ; Jeanne d'Orlay would never have pleaded for her unhappy son ; Sarah would certainly have been warned off *Hamlet* and would never have learnt *Lorenzaccio* ; the procession of Rostand's lyrics might have been robbed of much of their glory ; Princess Far-away might never have carried her crimson roses ; Izeyl would not have worn her orchid crown. And for his *Dame aux Camélias* Dumas would surely have looked in vain for a star to shine between La Doche and La Duse, and in sheer beauty to outshine them both. If on that April afternoon the Théâtre Français was impoverished, posterity was proportionately enriched.

The enterprising Mr. Jarrett at once leapt in ; the contract which he held out for an American tour and which Sarah signed without giving it a second thought, quoted five thousand francs for each performance with a stout percentage on profits over a certain sum, two thousand francs a week for hotel bills, and a special

---

[1] " Il faut voir Thérèse," said Sarah to Edmund Gosse, " c'est assommaut, mais c'est grand."

Pullman car for the journeys with a drawing-room, a piano, and two cooks. A hundred thousand francs was paid in advance, and with this in her pocket, thirty-six costumes in her imperials, and eight plays in her repertoire, Sarah sailed for America. The terms in question were looked upon as wholly fantastic ; Hollywood to-day would blush to offer them to any twinkling star in the film industry.

Sarah's first American tour differed little from those to follow, except that at the outset there was no little prejudice to overcome and a good deal of calumny to dissipate. But roughly, the first experience was always revived ; the reporters always clustered, the rapturous receptions were always reaffirmed, the prices usually established fresh records, and the money flowed like water through Sarah's open fingers. Is the same story true of life " in the studio " ? Perhaps so, but scarcely marked either by Sarah's generosity or by her genius.

CHAPTER V

MODJESKA

ON a Saturday afternoon in May 1880 another star suddenly shone out ; a Polish actress arrived at the Court Theatre and on the Monday her name was to be passed eagerly from lip to lip. The fame of Helena Modjeska[1] had already run through her native country and no less loudly through the United States, which she had toured. In London she had appeared at a party given by Mr. Hamilton Aidé—one of the first to blend artists with those whose only profession was to belong to the leisured classes. His guests, although a little uncertain as to whether a very attractive woman was repeating the Polish alphabet or reciting a poem, applauded her vigorously. Managers, however, were a little shy of the marked foreign accent, and it required perhaps courage as well as courtesy on the part of Wilson Barrett to offer the hospitality of the little theatre in Sloane Square on fifty-fifty terms. Modjeska wanted to be seen first as Marie Stuart, but the stage

[1] Her first husband's name was Modizejewski, which for stage purposes she simplified.

was voted too small and a rather thin version of *La Dame aux Camélias*, under the name of *Heartsease*, was selected. Many years earlier Modjeska had declined an offer which came from the author himself that she should enact his consumptive *Traviata*. From patriotic motives she refused to play in Germany, and she turned down Dumas's proposal because—although she would not say so—she had not sufficient money to buy the dresses requisite if she were to compete with her sisters in art in Paris. The French stage for a great many years set the fashion in clothes for every Parisian *élégante*, and even the great ladies from the Faubourg, who would perish rather than " have anything to do with " an actress, would eagerly copy the thought-out toilettes behind the footlights, every detail of which they drank in from their baignoires or avant-scenes. But by now Modjeska had some money ; she had played the " Dame " to frenzied enthusiasm in America,[1] she had visited and wept over the grave of the original Marie Duplessia, and was quite prepared to abide by the affable Wilson Barrett's advice. Her lover was impersonated by Arthur Dacre, a brawny rather than brainy actor whose subsequent lack of success drove him with his more gifted wife, Amy Roselle, to commit double suicide in Australia. One injunction was laid on him ; in America

[1] She made her cough so harrowing that in the West the miners believed she was really consumptive and sent her not only flowers but patent medicines.

at the end of the ballroom scene Armand had more than once wounded the actress's eye when throwing the gold coins in her face ; would Mr. Dacre kindly wait until Mme. Modjeska was on the floor face downwards before strewing his glittering coins over her ?

The title of the play too had its merits, for a certain number of mothers, only hearing of the startling success of a foreign actress and having missed the notices of the play, took their daughters to see it, believing they would find an adaptation of Miss Charlotte Yonge's novel, a book so intensely proper that John Keble begged the authoress to cut out, as being a little coarse, a phrase in which she alluded to the heart as something more than a mere engine for pumping blood. And if some of these worthy matrons were a little disconcerted by the theme, they could console themselves with the reflection that the pathos with which Modjeska invested the part left doubts as to whether Constance—so called in this version—could really have been so flagrant a sinner, and could anyhow comfort themselves with the assurance that she would certainly be among the saved.

" Go and hear Sarah say the letter she knows by heart in the last act of the *Dame aux Camélias*. It will be an object-lesson to you how to sustain the voice in the minor key." This was once the advice of the renowned

Madame Marchesi to a pupil whom she was training
for grand opera. Not only was Modjeska's intonation
perfect, but when she read the letter one felt that she
must know every syllable of it by heart, as she surely
could never have seen the lines through an obvious mist
of tears. For fourteen matinées and then for three
months of a regular engagement there were packed
houses at the Court. The Prince and Princess of Wales
had given the cachet of their presence at a début, the
Prince had at once caused the actress and her husband,
Count Chlapowski, to be presented, and through the
whole summer London besieged the box office for seats
and rained invitations on the Count and Countess—
who cared little for their title—for every sort of entertainment. They themselves entertained freely in the
hotel which occupied pride of place among the then
rather sorry inns in London, about to hang their heads
at the advent of such hostelries as the Savoy, the Ritz,
and the Carlton, which were to vie with one another in
attracting artists and others from across the water.

The invitations which perhaps pleased her most came
from Tennyson and Browning. The Poet Laureate,
whose behaviour was at times the reverse of polished,
read her some of his poetry and made her cry ; Browning knew a good deal about Polish art and Polish artists
and aired his knowledge with considerable freedom.
In Paris, Victor Hugo had " upset " Modjeska by saying bluntly that neither England nor America knew any-

thing about art ; the English poets took the same view as regards the United States, and she must now defend volubly, if not always quite intelligibly, the country of her adoption.

Marie Stuart—a combination of two translations from the German—followed hard on *Heartsease* and brought a different, a more serious, and an even more appreciative public.

Modjeska had evidently made a profound and highly sympathetic study of Mary's career and character ; she confessed to being " always slightly excited " when she spoke about the unhappy Queen. At Edinburgh she went again and again to Holyrood and scolded an attendant for selling a faked picture of Rizzio, while she was almost beside herself with anger when an American told her that Mary had borne a number of illegitimate children. *Marie Stuart* proved a great draw later in the provinces—as earlier in America—although the actress had often to complain of faulty stage arrangements. At Birmingham she declared that the limelights made Shrewsbury look like an orange and Elizabeth like a strawberry ice-cream, while on one unhappy occasion the lights themselves went out with a snap at the moment when she had to kneel before her haughty rival.

To the Court Theatre the Prince of Wales came several times ; like other members of the House of Hanover, he professed great sympathy for Mary of Scots and found " very refreshing " the big scene in which honours were shared with Miss Louise Moody, an old actress of the old school from whom it might not be amiss if some of the young actresses of the young school could take a wrinkle. The Prince would bring with him his favourite companion of the moment, a Polish nobleman, Count Jaracewski—familiarly known as Sherry-Whiskey—who taught the Prince to pronounce accurately the name of the actress's husband with its difficult Polish hard " i." *Marie Stuart* sealed Modjeska's reputation and, " Is this a real rival to the Sarah, whom we idolized last year ? " became a not inapt question, a question which increased in fervour when Adrienne Lecouvreur asserted herself in London as triumphantly as she had done in America. Those who could remember Rachel now drew on their memories and began to compare the Jewish tragedienne with the new-comer, who, by the way, was a very devout Catholic.

Then in the New Year a frost—a literal frost—set in. The weather was so bitter and the ground so hard that people would not take their horses out and clung to their own fireside. Cab-owners were almost equally shy, only one horse bus debouched on Sloane Square and scanty and shivering audiences were the result. To warm things up Barrett tried *Romeo and Juliet*. He cast Forbes-Robertson, then in the first flush of his success, as Romeo and himself as Mercutio, and gave a rendering which the arch critic of the day, Clement Scott, lauded to the skies. Modjeska was a lovely Juliet in every sense of the word, except that she was not quite mistress of the pronunciation of the words themselves ; this had been of no consequence as Adrienne and would prove of advantage as Odette, and, despite a really rather attractive disability, her notices were so uniformly flattering that pity it was she forgot how often *le mieux* is *l'ennemi du bien*, and insisted on the terms of her contract, under which she need not act the same play for more than fifty nights ; she forsook Juliet to play Juana, the gloomy heroine of one of Wills's least cheerful tragedies. Juana ran, or rather limped, for a very short while, but to mark the sense of their sister's superb art, a Benefit—not of the Snevellici sort—was arranged and Irving, the Bancrofts, the Kendals, Ellen Terry and Sarah Bernhardt herself took part.

Modjeska made one more appearance at the Haymarket Theatre a year later, in a problem play called *Odette*, which Sardou wrote when burning with indignation against the new divorce laws in France, of which an outraged husband could not avail himself.[1]

The conditions for divorce, if equally irreligious, differed sharply in this country, so that the play had to be twisted and the outraged husband—a rather dull fellow—

[1] Sardou tilted at the law with another play called *Divorçons*, in which the delightful Celine Chaumont—the French counterpart of Mrs. Bancroft—scored heavily at the Palais Royal.

must punish his wife by refusing to divorce her and thus prevent her from marrying her lover. The first act of *Odette* was a play in itself and left on one the not incorrect impression that the rest of it must be something of an anti-climax, an impression deepened by the fact that Odette did not appear at all in the second act and, after an exquisite scene with her daughter, finally committed suicide " off." The first curtain fell every night to a furore of applause, and the actress herself was often so overwrought by the thought of her infidelity, and the consequent separation from her child, that in the wings she would sob out : " Oh, what a naughty woman I am ! "

Odette ran for the season, which really then was the " season," and which closed with the precision of clockwork on the Saturday before Goodwood. Thanks largely to Modjeska, and partly to Charles Brookfield who made an immense hit in the small part of a major-domo at a Nice gambling-club, it proved a financial as well as an artistic success.

Bancroft was liberal, if never lavish, with his salaries. A story was current that, when an important member of the company asked for a rise from his weekly £20, he was met with : " I think you are perfectly justified ; you are a most valuable member of our company, and shall we say twenty-two pounds ? " For the first time now, a weekly salary at a West End theatre ran into three figures, and with bated breath it was whispered in the green-room that every "treasury night" Modjeska's cheque was for £100.

After this the London public saw Modjeska no more ; for twenty years she continued to play, but America —and more especially California, where she found her home—claimed all her work. England, to the loss of all theatre lovers, missed her Magda, her Katherine, her Norah, her Frou-Frou, her Lady Macbeth, and only heard of her soaring successes in them all. Just as Sarah disliked the part of Mrs. Clarkson in *L'Etrangère*, so Modjeska shrank from Peg Woffington and shirked, whenever possible, Lady Isabel in *East Lynne*.[1] She revolted against the jig with Triplet in which Mrs. Bancroft revelled, and she thought Mrs. Henry Wood's Lady Isabel a tame and undecided character ; the death-bed scene of Little Willie seemed to her rather shallow sob-stuff, and it was only in deference to her American manager's insistence and the demand of the American public that she allowed *East Lynne* to be part of her repertoire on tour. Perhaps no artist evoked quite so much solid admiration in the States, which she toured again and again ; the odious system of selling seats by

[1] *East Lynne* must have been played nearly a million times, but owing to the then absence of "copyright," Mrs. Henry Wood for a great many years never received a penny. The same in slightly lesser degree can be said of Miss Braddon's *Lady Audley's Secret*.

auction was in vogue, and to satisfy the demands of the box office she would often give ten performances in a week.

Juliet's dictum, " The more I give the more I have," was her motto ; and remembering her alike on the stage and in pleasant friendship, one remembers that she spared nothing and reserved nothing in her desire to give always of her best.

" To get out of myself," she wrote, " to forget all about Helena Modjeska, to throw my whole soul into the assumed character, to lead its life, to be moved by its emotions, thrilled by its passion, to suffer or rejoice, —in a word, to identify myself with it and reincarnate another soul and body ;—this was my ideal and at the same time the entrancement and attraction of my work."

It was a high ideal, perhaps an attempt at the impossible, but her failures were few, and like all honourable failures, might be vested with more merit than many of her startling triumphs. Admittedly the standard she set up for herself she tried to exact of others. " An actor," she would say, " must possess intelligence, quick perception, originality, a good deal of imagination, an expressive face, a fine figure, and a few other attributes not often summed up in one mortal man." She " tried," a pretty high trial, a good many leading men, and there is reason to think that the one who approached most nearly to her ideal was Johnston Forbes-Robertson, her Maurice de Saxe and her Romeo.

73

It was a time when " last appearances " and " positively last appearances " were in vogue, and not the least tribute to Helena Modjeska is to say that the moment she felt the first, and slightest, sense of failing power to hold her own, she caused the final curtain to fall on her.

CHAPTER VI

IRVING

"JE ne vous dis pas que c'est un très grand acteur mais c'est le plus grand artiste qu'il y ait au monde," said Sarah Bernhardt to a friend one evening at a house in Piccadilly, which she was thrilled to hear had once been occupied by Lord Byron.[1]

It was not due to anything like precocious criticism, or to any rash desire to challenge Lord Tennyson's dictum as to Henry Irving being better in the part than Macready, that, on seeing this great artist play Hamlet in 1879, I admitted to myself a feeling of disappointment. One may have been still smarting under a recent imposition of the tragedy as an Eton holiday task, one may have been too immature a playgoer to be capable of forming any opinion at all worth the name, one

[1] 139 Piccadilly, then the residence of Lord Glenesk, one of Sarah's closest friends. The house had belonged to the so-called wicked Duke of Queensberry, then to Lady Elizabeth Foster, afterwards Duchess of Devonshire, and later to the Byrons. It was here their only daughter Ada was born. Sarah was always specially interested to hear that Byron was supposed to have had the front door bricked up when he left.

75

may have been a little dismayed by certain physical dis-
abilities and marked mannerisms—the stamping gait,
the tendency to drag one leg, the peculiar pronunciation
—one may have been so absorbed by the delights of
Ellen Terry's appearance, of her every spoken word or
gesture, as to be unduly neglectful of everyone else in
the cast ;—anyhow, Forbes-Robertson, easily first among
Hamlets in the writer's rather large experience and humble
judgment, and in recent days John Gielgud and Maurice
Evans seemed to give one a clearer notion of the refine-
ment, the grace, the charm of a Sovereign's eldest son
than did the actor who overshadows them all. But
with every subsequent occasion—and they were very
many—one seized to watch the art of a man who had
leapt almost at a bound to a pinnacle where he seems
imperishably to stand, one's admiration for all that he
did, and dared, grew and grew until it reached fever
heat with the production—or perhaps even higher with
the last revival—of *Becket*.

Irving's hold on the public was perhaps never more
clearly shown than when, at Drury Lane, on an April
evening in 1905, he was "discovered" sitting rather
far back on the stage engaged in a game of chess with
King Henry. The whole house rose with a roar of wel-
come—with which sympathy was largely mingled, for
by then he had suffered sadly in health and wealth—and
some five minutes, or more, elapsed before turnultuous
greetings could be hushed and the play could be allowed

to proceed. *Becket* was perhaps Irving's greatest artistic, as it was certainly his greatest financial, triumph. He took three years after Tennyson's delivery of the script before deciding to put it on the stage ; it took only a few months for him to persuade the Poet Laureate to cut some slices out of the text and to write in a new speech for him at the end of the first act.

Almost with his last breath Tennyson said : " I suppose I shall never see *Becket*, but I can trust Irving ; he will do me justice." The poet was right : Irving did him a good deal more than justice. The difficulty of forming a good play out of a fine novel is a commonplace. In *Becket*, Irving did more ; he created a superb acting drama out of a very undramatic poem. Nor would he allow it to be a one-part play ; Genevieve Ward, an actress whose amazing powers were of a piece with her perfect " finish," William Terriss, Ellen Terry and others, all had full scope and a good deal more than fair play, but Irving stood out supreme. The master of statecraft, the worldling in his gorgeous lay robes, merged gradually, almost imperceptibly, into the Saint who, faithful unto death, in the moment of a violent death, could say his " Into Thy Hands " with utter and serene confidence.

All his faults—supposing them to be faults—of gait and diction, all the mannerisms—real or affected—were cast aside or disappeared ; every gesture was grandeur itself, every word was music to the ear.

No wonder that whenever *Becket* was in the bill, whether in London or the provinces, those who had not seen it before spoke of an experience which they could not easily match, those who had witnessed the performance once, hurried to witness it anew. No wonder Queen Victoria avowedly " wanted to see *Becket* " and, at the end of a memorable evening at Windsor, was outspoken to Irving and Ellen Terry as to the nobility both of the play and its rendering, with the graceful reminder that " it would have delighted Tennyson as much as it has delighted us." And those who knew, and cared for, Irving and knew him to be a simple Christian believer, were glad that the commendation should be the words which marked the close of his career, for there was to be but a bare half-hour between the death-scene on the stage at Bradford and the swift death of the actor himself.

Becket was first seen in 1893 ; two years later came an even more sensational, if less sustained, stroke of genius. Conan Doyle had written a one-act piece—why does one never see a one-act play now ?—which he called a *Straggler of '15*. Irving glanced through it, sent whatever cheque was asked, and for two years the typewritten sheets reposed in his desk. The opportunity for " presenting " the sketch came when *The Bells* was not thought a long enough bill of fare for a provincial tour, and at Bristol in the autumn of 1894 the re-named *Story of Waterloo* received the unanimous, and vociferous, applause

78

LETTER FROM HENRY IRVING

27 May 1895

not only of the local audiences, but of a force of London and American critics who had journeyed by special train for the event.

If Irving had too little thought for to-morrow, he certainly, as far as pecuniary considerations were concerned, had far less thought for himself. *Waterloo* was billed for a first performance at the Lyceum in conjunction with an adaptation of Don Quixote, and a large public was eagerly expecting to taste its merits.

Then came a message from a Royal lady—the mother of Queen Mary—a dear and devoted friend of the theatre in general, and of Irving in particular. " Would Mr. Irving play the *Story of Waterloo* at a special matinée in aid of the Newport Market Industrial Training School ? " No thought of taking the edge off the interest in a Lyceum production protruded itself ; the answer was an unhesitating " Yes " and accompanied by a cheque of £20 for a box which was placed at his disposal. There may be some who stand astride the last forty years to say that three happenings on the English stage are fixed in memory : Mrs. Kendal in the *Likeness of the Night*, Forbes-Robertson as Buckingham, and Irving when at the Garrick Theatre he played Corporal Brewster for the first time before a London audience. It was said that Conan Doyle wanted to paint in words and action what Hubert Herkomer would have depicted on canvas ; certainly he gave a portrait straight out of Chelsea Hospital. Grey, bent, and hungry for his rations, the old hero of the 3rd Guards still had the fire of battle in his veins, the smell of powder in his nostrils. He cried like a child over his broken pipe, but he stood up straight to attention when the Colonel came into the room. He could remember nothing which had happened that morning, but the tight corner in which the Scots Guards found themselves on the morning of that 18th of June was quite clear in his mind. He dozed like an old, old man in the armchair, but when he woke with a start to live again for a moment the great moment of all his days, " The Third Guards need powder and, by God, they shall have it " rang out with trumpet sound. It was the last effort of a life's battle stoutly fought, and when it died away one knew the 3rd Guards had their full muster in the unseen land.

When the curtain sank there was a silence, intensely significant but almost unbearable in its tension ; men who had never before been " moved by theatrical stuff " were furtively wiping their eyes, women were quite unashamedly " having a good cry," a wave of emotion swept the whole house, who by the way had paid pretty smartly for their seats. The stage manager knew his job and kept the drop down until people had a little recovered themselves and were able to give Irving an ovation which admittedly, in volume and sincerity, exceeded anything he had hitherto enjoyed.

The sketch was preceded by *The Vicarage*, in which Mrs. Bancroft, who was always susceptible to a house packed with notabilities, gave to the Vicar's wife all the tenderness of pathos and humour of which she was eminently capable. Perhaps, however, it was on account of the notabilities that she made the one little artistic blunder which can be traced to her. The stage direction, always closely observed, was that the old lady should be " discovered " playing draughts with her silver-haired husband ; for this occasion the actress, in order to secure a " reception," insisted on having an " entrance," and thus a very charming picture was lost.

Waterloo was followed by the rather noisy third act of *David Garrick*, but Charles Wyndham and Mary Moore ruefully confessed that, although they strove their hardest, their contribution to the afternoon's entertainment came as an anticlimax ; Irving had carried his audience so high that they could not drop down at once into broad comedy. Pinero, in one of his plays, insists that in the life of every individual there is one supreme hour which is never repeated ; it is possible to think that on a dark December afternoon Henry Irving as an actor had his hour. It is anyhow certain that in after years he constantly dwelt on it and that, as far as *Waterloo* was concerned, he never quite lived it again. *Waterloo* has always for its pendant, only a much showier pendant, Kipling's *The Man Who Was*, the post-Crimean episode in which Tree displayed himself at rather more than his very best. Both sketches present such outstanding opportunities, such colourful portraits, that one wonders why brilliant young actors with temperament like Mr. John Gielgud and Mr. Laurence Olivier have not made use of them.

And in the spring of 1895 there came the award which the recipient insisted was conferred on his "calling" (he disliked the term "profession") rather than on himself. Anyhow, the accolade which the Queen bestowed with the words, "I am very very pleased," was the first honour [1] conferred by a Sovereign, or a State, on an actor as such; for when Got was accorded the Legion of Honour, it came with the explicit reminder that it was as a professor he had been picked out.

Max Beerbohm, who happened to see Irving in his not very well-appointed brougham on his way to Paddington to take train for Windsor—"his hat tilted at more than its usual angle and his long cigar seemingly larger than ever"—amused himself by thinking what impression the new knight would make on the Sovereign, and was disposed to think it would be much the same as that stamped by Disraeli. Max perhaps forgot that the first opinion formed of Disraeli, and one which took a good many years to obliterate, was highly unfavourable. Perhaps he forgot also that the one loved colour and display

[1] Irving used to like the story that when the Press was first honoured and Mr. Borthwick was knighted, Lord Beaconsfield, in furtherance of a toast, rather derisively proposed to the "new knight," said in his most sententious tones : "Let us indeed drink to the health of Sir Algernon Borthwick, who shares his honour with Sir Isaac Newton and Sir Walter Raleigh."

largely because he thought they enhanced the art whose devoted servant he was ; in the case of the other they were part and parcel of the Orientalism which was so large an ingredient in Disraeli's character. And by a curious change in their parts it so happened that, in the private circumstances of life, the actor had far fewer " affectations " than the statesman.

" What are you going to do next ? " said Albert Edward, Prince of Wales, to Irving early in 1882, and on being told that *Romeo and Juliet* was to be the new venture there came in all good faith the exclamation : " Most interesting ; who will play Romeo ? " The question, if a little unfortunate, had its justification, for the love-sick boy was really as unsuited to Irving's temperament as to his physique. Romeo, whatever his charm, is as irresponsible as he is hot-headed, and perhaps the reason why Irving and Forbes-Robertson never shone at their brightest in the part, is because a sense of responsibility is to be found at the base of both their characters.

But apart from this little slip Irving's relations with Edward VII were of the happiest, and that monarch left it on record that of all the plays he had seen—and they must have numbered many hundreds—*The Corsican Brothers* afforded him the most enjoyment. The first congratulations on the knighthood came from Marlborough House ; at the suppers on the Lyceum stage Albert Edward was no infrequent guest, and at Sandringham, Irving, in *The Bells* and a scene from *The Merchant*, was the bridge over which Queen Victoria passed from complete aloofness with regard to theatrical doings to renewed and something like keen interest in them.

The survivors of the famous costume ball at Devonshire House—and we are not many—will perhaps remember, more than anything else, Henry Irving as he strode through the rooms in his rose-red Cardinal Wolsey's robes. Was there a little squeeze of lemon-juice in his remark to the Prince of Wales, gorgeously arrayed as a Knight of Malta : " These ladies and gentlemen are very fine but they do not seem to have got quite inside their characters."

Of all his costumes Irving preferred Wolsey's robes to any other. He had no personal vanity—the peacock and he were as the poles apart—but he was too clever not to know that not even as Hamlet or Charles I, characters favoured by the portrait painter, did he appear to such advantage as in his dominating part in *Henry VIII*. He went to an enormous expenditure of time, trouble and money for the costumes for this play ; month in, month out, assistants bent their heads at the South Kensington Museum making coloured drawings of period stuff ; looms worked overtime to produce these stuffs for the costumiers ; material of real cloth of gold at ten guineas a foot was submitted for inspection and only rejected because found ineffective ; Irving's own robe was an exact reproduction of one lent to him by a famous painter, and an artist was despatched to Rome to try, but to try in vain, to get the old tint. To any remonstrance on the score of extravagance was offered the laconic reply : " When you are getting into the skin of a character you must not neglect the wardrobe."

" Full compliments and 'alf rations, Bill," murmured a jaded pursuer of De Wet in the weary South African warfare after a congratulatory message had been read out in camp and a short supply of " bully " and biscuit tendered. Scarcely had the last echo of congratulations, pouring in from every corner of the world, died away when the tide of fortune set in against " Sir Henry." Early in 1896 he injured his knee and many months elapsed before he could face the footlights again ; the drama about Peter the Great, written by his son, and *The Medicine Man* from the pen of Hichens, were costly failures ; his immense stock of scenery was accidentally burnt, and he had to sell his fine library and transfer his interest in the Lyceum Theatre to a company. Lastly, Sardou's *Dante*, produced at Drury Lane, proved wholly unprofitable, and although, both here and in America, Irving rightly remained on the pedestal to which a discriminating public had hoisted him, it was a sick and sorrowful man who undertook in the autumn of 1905 his last provincial tour and to an eager and enthusiastic Bradford audience he recorded his last *adsum*.

It would savour of impertinence for a mere hack play-goer to attempt any appreciation, or criticism, of an artist who seems to grow in stature as he recedes into history. But remembering him—and who could forget him—in something like half a hundred of those representations he so richly offered, remembering him as a man whose heart was as warm as his brain was quick, as a friend who never swerved from his friendships, as a host, or guest, delightful in talk with a charm magnetic for men younger and less distinguished than himself, and with a wit which gave no wound, remembering him under these and under many other lights, one reminds oneself that take him for all in all, one never quite saw his like in this London of ours.

"I remember in the days of my youth," said Mr. Asquith when unveiling the tribute to Beerbohm Tree, " when Mr. Gladstone was at the height of his fame and was often called the ' Idol of the Nation,' that a shrewd observer once said, ' If you were to take a plebiscite as to who was the most popular man in England, he would be easily beaten by Dr. W. G. Grace,' and I cannot help thinking that he would have found a most formidable competitor in Henry Irving."

CHAPTER VII

MRS. KENDAL[1]

FOR something like forty years two actresses stood
pre-eminent—coequal and nearly coeval—in the
sisterhood of the art of which they were proud to be
members. They were as twin towers, even of height, if
differing sharply in form ; their supremacy was un-
hesitatingly admitted, and to have denied it would have
been to depreciate English acting as a whole.

Said a French critic of Georges Sand : " *Il faut bien
qu'un roman se rapproche de la poésie ou de la science.*" There
have been some to aver that Ellen Terry represented the
poetry, Madge Kendal the science, of the craft ; yet
Ellen Terry's romance was fortified by serious study and a
very great deal more technique than appeared on the
surface, while Madge Kendal had but to read aloud a few

---

[1] Since this chapter was ready for press Dame Madge Kendal has
passed into the Silent Land. Her most apt and most brilliant pupil,
Sir Seymour Hicks, wrote some lines about her in the " Daily
Mail " on the morrow of her falling asleep which all should read
who revere her memory and wish to understand something of the
arcana of her life.

lines of Byron or Swinburne for her hearers to be assured that the essence of poetry was an ingredient in the blood that coursed through her veins. There comes, as one writes, rather dim, if wholly delightful, recollections of the *Palace of Truth*, *Broken Hearts*, and a charming comedietta, *Uncle's Will*. But at whatever age one saw Madge Kendal—the name trips off one's tongue—enact Galatea, neither Time nor Circumstance could efface it from memory.

W. S. Gilbert's fertile brain had devised the fragrant fantasy, he was content that a still very youthful actress should furnish it from an inexhaustible store of imagination combined with, at her age, an almost uncanny knowledge of her business. In a flawless performance one little point seems sometimes to stick out for observation. It was often said that Madge Kendal could do more with the flick of an eyelid than anyone else could suggest with a movement of the whole head. The first and last moments of the Statue were a flutter of the eyelids ; the first indicated the inflowing of life, the last was the action which had the heartrending " Farewell, Pygmalion, farewell " for its accompaniment. Was it perhaps here and now that the actress discovered how telling a flick or flutter of the eyelids could be ?

The whole conception, no less than the execution, of the part—the latter at times half-dreamy, at others wholly vivacious—proved that this country could put up a powerful rival to famous *ingénues* such as Mademoiselle

Dudley and Mademoiselle Reichemberg, both about to become stars at the Comédie ; what was even more difficult, there was provoked the unstinted approval of the author who admittedly was not over prone to praise.

With Galatea, Dame Madge Kendal—the title under which generations of playgoers will do her homage—gave a foretaste of what she could, and would, do on either side of the Atlantic ; with Galatea she established a position from which there has never been any attempt to dislodge her. Her Galatea also made good another point of first-rate importance. William Kendal's performance of Pygmalion went to show that her determination to play with no one else than her husband opposite her was founded on solid dramatic, as well as other, reasons.

Early in 1875 a combination was formed of John Hare, who, introduced to London by Mrs. Kendal's brother, Tom Robertson, had since made for himself a name, and the Kendals ; the three put themselves down for weekly salaries of £25 : one wonders at what figure artists of their calibre would estimate their services in any theatrical enterprise to-day.

It is within just surmise that Pinero wrote both *The Money Spinner* and *The Squire*, if not for Mrs. Kendal, anyhow holding her forward in his mind : with the latter the Kendal Hare Management touched the zenith of its success, and at least 75 per cent of that success was due to the interpretation of the title rôle. The Squire in the earlier scenes, in her print dress and beautifully " got-up " linen collar and cuffs—a dress no less thought-out because it was simplicity itself—so entirely suggested, and caused the whole Company to suggest, all that was meant by English country life that every scene was said to " waft the scent of the hay across the footlights."

In the second act of *The Squire* Mrs. Kendal wore a dress with gold threads running through it on which the fire could play when she consigned to the flames the cherished correspondence with real tears running down her cheeks and with perhaps her most poignant stage cry : " There is no warmth in burnt love-letters." Not the least of the details of her art was her insistence on dressing not so much for the audience as for the occasion. Thus in the first act of *Diplomacy*, if Julian is to believe in Dora's perfect chastity, he must not see her in the fashions of the Rue de la Paix or the Rue Royale ; the dress worn by the original Dora before her betrothal was perfectly made but gave the idea that it was home-made.

The British playgoers paid a rather heavy penalty for the success of *The Squire* as it led, if not immediately, to the translation of the Kendals to America for no inconsiderable period. When they finally returned towards the close of the last century there were some to ask themselves rather anxiously whether any of the bloom or

delicacy of Mrs. Kendal's art could have been brushed off ;
alike in New York and in stumping the States it was felt
that she may have had to make broader and harder strokes
with her brush than at the Court or at the St. James's.
She was to belie once and for all any such sinister suggestion, and at the familiar house in King Street she found
her first vehicle in *The Elder Miss Blossom* ; it was a play
" run up " by a clever member of the Company with
about as little stagecraft and as many perfect human
touches as would be found thirty years later in *Journey's
End*. The story was quite simple ; an explorer, absent
from England for some years, had been captivated by a
photograph and entered into a love correspondence, but
mistakenly with the maiden aunt instead of the young
niece. Dorothy Blossom's unconscious rival was the
child she had adopted and adored, the motherless
daughter of her favourite brother. In the second act
(why are second acts always the strongest ?) the actress
had one of those chances which she never failed to seize.
Dorothy was no " old maid " but a woman of heart and
brain and beauty who had become deeply enamoured of
the hero whose presentment she had cherished through
three long years, and who, she believed, could satisfy her
own craving for a good man's love. And now she must
eat her heart out, as it were, crush her wholly natural
impulse, and blot from her sight the man she had taught
herself to worship. There were displayed all the dignity,
all the sweetness of a disappointed woman ; " It came so

late, the love that so many girls treat with indifference would have been the joy and the substance of my life," was the burden of a wail she could not stifle ; only one thing she would ask, " Don't, don't laugh at me," and the less than half a dozen words spoken with smiling lip and a voice which strove to be steady constituted as pathetic a petition as one has ever heard offered on the stage.

I believe there are actresses still among us who went more than once to study Mrs. Kendal's methods and effects in the scene which was to have a happy, though perfectly artistic, ending. Every chord of feminine feeling was touched with sureness but with infinite delicacy ; every emotion was there but each one was mastered ; the tears were in the eyes but a proud woman somehow kept them from falling ; relief was sought in a semblance of humour and in an attempt to mask with assumed indifference a bitter grief. Students, however young, would know that all this—and there was a great deal more—was the result of study, experience, insight into character, and behind these was the artistic temperament which no teaching can give. Rightly did the representative of a leading journal write : " Mrs. Kendal showed the brothers and sisters in art what the very best kind of English acting is ; and when English acting is good, it is of the very best."

Dorothy Blossom might very well have been thought to have exploited all the resources of an experienced

Tragedy —
looking at
Comedy
1865

DAME MADGE KENDAL

[*Facing p.* 92

actress's art ; Mrs. Kendal was to give one more exhibition of even greater worth.

In Mrs. Clifford's *Likeness of the Night* Mrs. Kendal deliberately chose the part of an uncongenial, unimaginative, puritanically minded wife who had brought her husband a fortune but was unable to be a mother. Never were mobile features called into requisition with more effect than in the moment when Mildred Acheson discovers that her husband, whom she secretly adores, has a mistress and one who has borne him the children denied to her. " The children " ; here was the crux of the wife's agony in the scene with her rival—admirably played by Lady Tree—and through the long duel of words, working up to her " God knows, and He will judge between us," Mrs. Kendal's eyes were again and again fixed on the toys, battered little objects, the sight and thought of which seemed to tear the heart from her breast. In the third act, in the saloon of the outward-bound liner, the actress grasped perhaps her last opportunity of showing what she could do under the stress of emotion which she was striving to curb or conceal. It was not amiss that the last passionate words which many of us heard her speak composed the cry to the husband who had so entirely misread her, " Take me in your arms once more." But the solid contribution which Mrs. Kendal could make to a play may be measured by the fact that she dominated the last act of *The Likeness of the Night* in which she herself did not appear ; one watched the coming and going of the guests at the party given by Bernard Acheson and the " lady " he had now married ; one heard without surprise the story of the steward who brought the letter which showed that Mildred had set a term to the life, which had been one long gnawing heartache, by throwing her body into the sea, one seemed to care very little that the new Mrs. Acheson, horror-struck, bade her husband " Stand back, between us flows the sea " ; the dull, drab woman had, apparently without effort, made her way into the innermost thoughts of the audience, and for many a long day the audience would find it difficult to dislodge her from them.

" Mrs. Kendal," wrote a frequenter of the theatre in Paris, somewhat prejudiced against the theatre in London, " has given a piece of acting which few French actresses in my long experience could rival, and none could surpass."

To mark the Coronation year of King Edward, the Trees, Ellen Terry and Mrs. Kendal romped joyously through the *Merry Wives*. In Shakespeare's famous farce Mrs. Kendal, with the exception of a few performances at the St. James's Theatre, made her last and grandest curtsey to the London public. For two or three years she toured the provinces and suburbs and then, without fuss and with the minimum of publicity, she left the stage and would be deaf to any entreaties to appear any more.

So much for the artist ; in pointing to her as a teacher, is it allowable to indulge in a military simile ? There have not been wanting writers to peck at the reputation of the soldier who led a vast British army to victory, but there has been no one to deny that Douglas Haig was the incarnation of good Staff work. There have been some to suggest that Mrs. Kendal had her limitations, that despite her faultless intonation, her infinite resource, she was never quite so happy in costume—with the solitary exception of Lady Clancarty—as when portraying the maid or matron in modern life ; no critic, however severe or even unfriendly, could be found to deny that she was the most absolute mistress of her art who, during nearly three generations, has faced the footlights in this country.

May one draw another military parallel and compare the modes of the great Moltke and Napoleon when giving orders ? Moltke started from the assumption that his subordinates had an intelligent and working knowledge of their business ; his orders were always helpful because they gave all the news available without prescribing to the recipient the procedure which he ought to consider and determine for himself. The helplessness and gaucherie of Napoleon's Marshals was often the consequence of their Imperial Master's method of intruding too much into the details which should have been left to the men on the spot. Mrs. Kendal always took the wise course at rehearsal of saying to members of her company : " At the beginning of a speech you should be in a certain place ;

at the end of it in another ; think out, and work out, for yourself how to get from one point to another." This was surely good generalship ; the orders were explicit but required those who received them to be mentally alert and use their own brains in carrying them out. Professional zeal and almost cloistered notions of self-discipline rendered her rigorous with herself and disinclined to be less exacting [1] with others. Those who worked with her must accept her standard and anyhow try to reach her ideals. And in the years during which she would be a spectator, good workers never lacked her approval, good advice has always been available for the asking, and a meed of glowing praise has often been offered. In the years ahead " Madge Kendal's " claim to be remembered will not be limited to a record of the parts she played with consummate skill ; to her honour will it be said of her that she founded a school and that—perhaps quite unconsciously—her pupils multiply with every year.

The question was once asked of Bartet why her acting

[1] That the strictness later hardened into something like intolerance is undeniable, and the intolerance crystallized into an abhorrence of modern methods and especially of modern dress, or the lack of it. " Let me know," she wrote to a dear friend, " the day you come for rest and quiet. *No clo!*—change for Evening meal—to *clean* blouse—same hair, same teeth—knees well covered—no rouge—no lipstick of *any shade*, when dressed you keep your clothes *ON*, only taking them off for bed—where you will be *alone*. I do not care for the knitted caps as worn in these days of super progress and super civilization—eyebrows not to be plucked out—or eyelashes lengthened—it is best not to try and correct your *Creator*. Love, MADGE."

remained on the same high level, whereas Marthe Brandés, who had been her peer at the Comédie, had dropped back a little when she transferred herself to the Boulevards. The answer was simple ; she had nothing but her art to think of ; " *les recettes ne me regardent pas.*" Mrs. Kendal insisted that her husband—a shrewd man of business, a loyal English gentleman, and a very sound actor withal—should charge himself entirely with the business end of the theatre. The stage was her demesne, and to the acting of her company and herself she could give her whole mind and thought and expert care.

In any play produced by her—and she was always her own producer—it was evident that the phrasing and gestures and costumes of each member of the Company had been as carefully considered, and considered as important as her own. " Never play a part," she said once to a rising young actor, " unless you feel it is going to take something out of you." The word of counsel was her own *mot d'ordre,* for the parts which exhausted her were the parts she liked best. The greater the demand on her the fuller the response, and to make that response she would, year in, year out, sacrifice much that many folk consider indispensably pleasant in daily life.

" To all I say work, and with enthusiasm " : such was Dame Madge Kendal's vale to her brothers and sisters of the stage, and if the words were written when the pen was beginning to loosen in the writer's grasp the advice is surely of sovereign value.

97   G

CHAPTER VIII

ELLEN TERRY

"WHAT does it matter," said a "celebrity" to a persistent journalist, "where I was born? What matters is what people say and think of me when I die." It matters very little whether Ellen Terry's birthplace is rightly assigned to a haberdasher's shop in Coventry ; it matters very much that when she drew her last breath, a vast public uncovered in affectionate salute.

Ellen Terry has lent herself both to portraiture and to biography. Sargent was only one of many who traced for us her beauty, a beauty which was well compared to a Veronese portrait, while Jules Claretie declared that she looked "like a living model of Giovanni Bellini" ; three or four substantial volumes, one from her own pen, have set out her story, but just as no painter could transfer to canvas all that was most fascinating in her features, so no chronological table of theatrical achievements or catalogue *raisonné* of theatrical merits could suffice to solve the secret of her art for which, anyhow in this country, no precise parallel can be found ; "*Humani nihil a me*

DAME ELLEN TERRY

[*Facing p.* 98

alienum," wrote a heathen poet and humanity was the
book always open to Ellen Terry. Yet she was an actress
from first to last and from head to foot, and she was
proud of it. The word "realism" would mean little
or nothing to her because the theatre was to her a reality ;
private lives lived within walled houses would—many
and many of them—have for her a much more pronounced flavour of sham. And the love of her art was
the measure of her unselfishness in conveying it ; the
play, and not her share in it, was the matter of cardinal
importance. So every detail of every play was thought
out ; she would hold an inquest on the characteristics
of every character. There was not only in question all
that could be done with Hermione or Ophelia or Lady
Macbeth ; it was a matter to her of equal concern how
Florizel should approach Perdita, how Hamlet should
address his mother, how Macduff should look when
Macbeth said this or that to him.

Controversy is still apt to rage round Ellen Terry's
Lady Macbeth, and comparisons are instituted between
her and Ristori, although few of us are now left who saw
Ristori play the part—alas, to a rather thin, cold audience
—at Drury Lane. Giulia Ristori's high dramatic instinct
was mated to a keen intellectual study—truly remarkable
in the child of strolling players—in respect of which she
was probably ahead of any of her sisters in art. To the
great declamatory parts of the Italian actress her English
sister could lay no claim any more than to Sarah's *voix*

d'or, but at least one can say that those who only saw a
regally beautiful queen in her peacock draperies, as perhaps Sargent only saw her, have missed the woman
whose firm touches from end to end of the drama were a
superb foil to her lord's cowardice and who, with every
word and movement, pointed the tragedy of a great love
freely spent, however unworthily bestowed.

The cheap charge levelled against Ellen Terry was her
too often inability to remember her words. How far this
was a positive physical disability, how far it was due to
lack of concentration, can scarcely be determined. But
quite certainly any lack of concentration was due to her
seeing too much. Of Arthur Balfour it was said that, as
a statesman, he had great difficulty in registering a
decision because he saw so clearly both sides of an
argument. Ellen Terry saw the whole play spread out, as
it were, before her, but perhaps rather as in a picture
than as in a plan ; it needed special effort to absorb herself
in any particular section of it. Her selflessness as an
artist was part of her woman's character, and she was
always a woman with all a woman's sweet wilfulness.
Here was the source of any unconventionality in her life
and it was her weaker side ; her strong side, which was
far more often uppermost, was the quality that she
stamped on Shakespeare's heroines when, for our benefit,
she gave them the character many of us had hitherto
missed. Never too was there a more delicious compound
of joyousness and gentleness, a blend which forbade any

sense of vindictiveness. Lord Macaulay is sure that before praising anyone for an act of forgiveness, one must inquire whether the person is above or below revenge. With Ellen Terry one would not go into such niceties ; she would freely forgive almost before the offence was committed. Hers was a sweetness of nature which sufferings and troubles only seemed to render sweeter and sweeter still.

When Violet Vanbrugh—whose artistic worth and work Ellen Terry was quick to see and urge on others— was rehearsing Queen Katharine, the older woman went on the stage and reminded her that there must be no suggestion of scolding in the exposition of the Royal Lady's wrongs ; Katharine, she said, would be too dignified, too sorrowful, and withal too gentle, to scold. Precisely the same could be said of herself. " Duty so soon tires, Love goes all the road," says the Stranger in *The Third Floor Back* ; surely, if all unknowingly, Ellen Terry took Jerome's line for her own motto.

She was married, if marriage be the word, when she was sixteen ; and she rebelled—there was always something of the rebel in her—and rushed off with the man she loved, and him, and the children she bore him, she loved to the end. But from her lips there fell no word of bitterness, only words of tender regret, about the great artist who plucked too quickly at a youthful flower, and whose devotion could never fill her life. " Ellen Terry was *never* immoral," said that splendid Georgina,

Lady Salisbury, with honest indignation ; " she was only rather illegal."

Amid all the figures, dramatic, poetic, romantic, medieval or comparatively modern which crowd to mind or memory, no two persons ever seem quite to agree which was Ellen Terry's " best Shakespearean part." There are some to assert that she seems only to have touched absolute perfection in Portia and Beatrice, others stoutly maintain that in Cordelia, Imogen and Hermione was more manifest her ability to say simple things with a perfect simplicity which tugged at the heartstrings. Her Ophelia was infinitely studied, it was said under Irving's guidance, with the result that the mad scene, in which she really was mad, had, with each outburst, a meaning which underlined the whole story. One of the many compensations of old age is that one saw Ellen Terry's Portia just sixty years ago when she was herself twenty-seven, the age which Portia might well be supposed to be. When she played it again very much later on there was the same graciousness which never forsook her, the same effervescent mirth, the same satisfaction in bringing the truth to light, but the memory was already impaired, and there was a little lack of that exuberant vitality of youth, so exuberant as perhaps to be partly responsible for the restlessness of old age. And as one muses on her Olivia, perhaps the loveliest treasure she ever disclosed to us, her

Henrietta Maria, her Queen Katharine, one is tempted to wonder whether the theatre lost a little from her unswerving loyalty to Henry Irving. When the partnership was severed the early autumn of life had set in ; the ill-starred season at the Imperial Theatre was to do something to depress even her mercurial spirits, Lady Cicely in *Captain Brassbound's Conversion* and *Alice Sit by the Fire* were not perhaps the parts she would have chosen had she been her own manager earlier on. It was probably with eagerness that she accepted Tree's offer, backed by a substantial honorarium, to let a later public be infected by the joyousness—the word bears repetition—with which she could indifferently vest Mistress Page or Mistress Ford. The story ran that she and Mrs. Kendal tossed up—or, more probably, asked someone else to toss up—and let the coin decide which part each should play. Mistress Page forgot many of her words, Mistress Ford remembered them all. Mistress Page was sometimes rather disconcertingly vague about her business as to which Mistress Ford was entirely sure. But people who saw Ellen Terry for the first time, foreigners who came to London attracted by the Coronation festivities, went back home asking themselves, a little bewilderedly, what precise quality it was which enabled an actress, already a sexagenarian, to charm them tenfold more than any other actress had ever been able to do.

Sarah Bernhardt's one failure was as Dona Clorinde in *L'Aventurière*. Although she by no means resented

Bernard Shaw's " How capitally vulgarly Sarah did " the reception of Von Keller in Magda. " Vulgarity is the one fault I never have had and never shall have," was her heated retort to a hostile critic. Ellen Terry's one misfire was in *Madame Sans-Gene* ; vulgarity and she were as the poles apart ; the simple Laundress was well within her wide range, the parvenue Duchess lay just outside it.

One thing is irrefutably true ; no actress was ever so beloved by her public as was Ellen Terry. Sarah Bernhardt and Elena Duse provoked admiration which again and again crossed the frontier of enthusiasm ; Ellen Terry, but little behind them in sheer efficiency, knocked at the hearts of her audience, and the door was opened without question or delay. Ruskin wrote of all the energies of men, " being awakened in the pursuit of beauty in the endeavour to arrest it or re-create it for themselves." Was this the keynote of the woman whose energies were continually awakened in the pursuit of the beauty which was her ideal, and whose genius lit up her whole path to fame. The path she chose was not always the easiest and sometimes not the safest, but she pursued it steadily to her last hour ; surely those who loved her here may think that she has found her lodging where " in the Home of Beauty all things of Beauty meet."

One other word cannot be repressed. Had the span of life for Ellen, and her scarcely less gifted sister, Marion, been extended but a few years, they would have seen the Terry traditions carried on at their highest level. They would have seen a young man, still young in years though already ripe in experience, playing part after part with swift master strokes, with delicate humour, with utter dignity. This would have meant very much to them, but perhaps even more would have been the knowledge that it is hard work in pursuance of his art which occupies every corner of John Gielgud's mind and every moment of his life, that he realizes—as they surely did—that whatever enhances the quality of that work must be carefully considered, whatever might tend to hamper or mar it must be ruthlessly cast aside.

CHAPTER IX

SOME BEAUTIFUL WOMEN

LADY HOLLAND (1810–89) declared that during a period of over forty years she had seen all the really beautiful women in Europe and that—not even excepting the seemingly peerless Lady Dudley—the only one she could remember as being absolutely faultless from the crown of her head to the sole of her foot was Cavour's emissary to the Court of Napoleon, Countess Castiglione, who passed the last thirty years of her life in absolute seclusion so that no one should see her waning looks.

"There is nothing," wrote Addison, "that makes its way more directly to the soul than beauty which immediately diffuses a secret satisfaction and complacency to the imagination." Certainly the beauty, even if not "absolutely faultless," of five English actresses who spring to happy recollection—Mrs. Rousby, Adelaide Neilson, Mrs. Langtry, Mary Anderson, and Gladys Cooper—have diffused satisfaction which was anything but secret. Mrs. Rousby and Mrs. Langtry, if one remembers the not inconsiderable successes they scored —the former especially in Tom Taylor's *Betwixt Axe and*

Crown—certainly found their faces an indispensable passport to their fame. Adelaide Neilson had a large repertoire, she gained a deservedly high reputation, and she enjoyed an amazing measure of popularity ; she was also a most agreeable acquaintance with no trace of affectation or pose, and there may be still one or two of us left to remember delightful morning rides with her in the Park in her early youth. But if she added distinct histrionic qualities to rare physical advantages, Adelaide Neilson—whose real name was Elizabeth Ann Brown— never wholly reached the art of concealing art and, though devoid of any vestige of jealousy, she was just a little self-conscious in drama and more than a little inclined to over-act in comedy. It is no figure of speech to say that for many years she was literally the talk of the town ; she had worked in a mill, she had served behind the bar in a public house, but that was as dust in the balance of her beauty and lovableness. She was asked everywhere, she might have married into the peerage, artists pleaded to be allowed to paint her, but what pleased her most was that when she played Juliet, the balcony scene was occasionally held up by the gallery boys blowing resounding kisses at her.

Mary Anderson and Gladys Cooper must stake their claims on the solid terrain of dramatic ability ; physical attractions here were to be matched with artistic achievements of no mean degree.

Mary Anderson, the heroine of Mrs. Humphry

Ward's *Miss Bretherton*, set the town talking in 1883 when the report of her dazzling beauty drew folk of all ages to the Lyceum Theatre and where her charm as Parthenia compelled them to sit through three acts of a cumbersome drama, *Ingomar*,[1] the women spectators being perhaps gratified to see a rude chieftain tamed by a gentle maiden.

Her Pauline in the *Lady of Lyons* was a careful, conscientious study, and showed a first-rate knowledge of stage business ; her graceful and intelligent movements as Galatea, her purity and clarity of intonation, and the ease with which she wore her classic costume, excited further, and warmer, admiration. But in the last two parts she must challenge the then fairly recent record of Mrs. Kendal, and it was not to disparage the stranger within our coasts if others besides journalists maintained that the Englishwoman stood unapproached and perhaps unapproachable in characters she had made specially her own.

Of course no actress so young, with such looks and such gifts as Mary Anderson, could forgo an opportunity which presented itself in the winter of 1884 of " doing "

---

[1] *Ingomar*, however, contained some pretty verses of rather cloying sweetness, the prettiest of which ran :

> And whence comes Love ? like morning's light
> It comes without thy call.
> And how dies Love, a spirit bright ?
> Love never dies at all.

(Photo by W. & D. Downey)

Mary Anderson de Navarro

MRS. STIRLING AND MARY ANDERSON

[Facing p. 108

Juliet, a bold essay, especially as it was to take place at
the Lyceum Theatre where only a couple of years earlier
Ellen Terry had ravished audiences in every one of the
lovely love scenes.[1]

Some of the critics, apparently still resenting an
American intrusion, were by no means friendly in their
notices and alluded faintly to a, wholly imaginary,
American accent. Lord Lytton, scarcely less famous as
an author than as an ambassador, rushed to the rescue.
Just as Mr. Gladstone's searching article in the " Nineteenth Century " sent everybody to their libraries and
booksellers to ask for *Robert Elsmere*, so Lord Lytton's
closely argued paper in the same monthly packet drew
a multitude of thoughtful men and women to judge for
themselves of a notable production, and more especially
to compare Mary Anderson with Ellen Terry whom most
of them had seen, and Helen Faucett of whom many of
them had read.

That Mrs. Stirling's Nurse was a masterpiece, alike in
its vigour and reality, admitted of no doubt, though it
gave no answer to the vexed question why that delightful
domestic should be represented as approaching her

[1] Just thirty years later Ellen Terry's niece played Juliet at the
New Theatre. Dame Madge Kendal was much struck by the merits
of the performance and aptly said to a friend : " Write down in
your pocket-book that you saw Phyllis Terry play Juliet in 1912
when she was only eighteen ; otherwise twenty years hence you will say
that you saw her play the part in this year and that probably she was
about twenty-three at the time."

dotage, whereas in real life she would be a woman of less than forty summers.

In one of his more perverse moods W. S. Gilbert delivered himself, to me, of the opinion that " Shakespeare often wrote d——d bad plays," and proceeding from the general to the particular he underlined at full length how impossible it seemed to him to cast satisfactorily a Romeo. The sweeping assertion about Shakespeare could be taken with several grains of salt ; the difficulty about a Romeo was irrefutable.

A short while ago an important American manager travelled to London in search of a lover for a very special Juliet. Where, he inquired, could he find precisely what he wanted ? The answer was, anyhow to the casual observer, so obvious that it was difficult to understand why the question was put, or why the " search " could not have been satisfied by a cable. It is possible to think that if William Shakespeare could rise from his grave and visit the theatres in London he would point to Laurence Olivier[1] as the model he required for the part. Features, figure, colour, quality of voice, eagerness of temperament, impetuosity of manner, high spirits veined by a characteristic melancholy, a rather unusual wealth of gesture, entirely appropriate to a hot-headed lovesick Italian boy, a power of expressing youthful passion apparently without restraint, yet never over-

[1] Since writing this chapter Laurence Olivier has been engaged to play Romeo at the New Theatre.

stepping the line ;—these are some of the attributes
which persuade one to point with steady finger to a
young actor, who so far has laudably withstood gilded
offers from the films, and to say "there is your
Romeo."

That William Terriss "looked a picture"[1] as Romeo
and bore himself superbly, especially in the last act, was
a verdict not to be gainsaid ; that he was lacking in
boyishness was a charge not easily refuted ; his high
spirits were said to be void of spontaneous gaiety, his
low spirits were rather those of a mature mourner than
of an impressionable stripling : it was a sound, if not a
seductive, performance. Anyhow, there was no fear of
any lapses such as occurred when Mary Anderson first
played Juliet at Louisville ; the leading man who had
played Romeo before she was born, not only forgot his
part but, what was worse, forgot the dagger and Juliet
had to stab herself with a hairpin.

As regards Juliet, the reports which reached the present
writer, greatly interested though actually engaged in
distant desert warfare, spoke of the young actress displaying a depth and tenderness of feeling which even
her immediate forerunner had not wholly achieved ; the
master touches of pathos rightly reached their climax
when in the final scene, having fallen a little distance

[1] The picture may have been recalled by many who witnessed
Jean de Retzke's torch-bearing entrance into the vault with his
incomparable *salut aux morts.*

from the body of her lover, she crept softly up to him and gently lifting his arm, placed it round her neck, nestling her head into the fold of it, to draw, with an exquisite sigh of satisfaction, her last breath.

There was one bit of business which appealed specially to any who saw the play with observant eyes. When the servant announced the arrival of the guests to the ball, music was faintly heard from the hall beyond. Catching the sound of this music Juliet, who had been paying scant attention to the talk between her mother and the Nurse, made a little dance movement with her feet as she followed Lady Capulet to the ballroom. It was as if her whole being were stirred by the irresistible impulse of a young creature whose instinct is to dance when she hears dance music and whose enjoyment of the ball would consist in the actual dancing, without any special interest in the dancers. The childishness shown at this point—a childishness which has escaped so many Juliets—made more real the womanliness evident in the second balcony scene when the woman's arms are about her lover and the embrace with which she clings to him should be that of a wife, even if only a girl wife.

Mary Anderson was explicit in her view that from the moment Juliet is convinced of her love for Romeo, she becomes a woman capable of any courageous, or even hazardous, action. The transition to womanhood was cunningly led up to by a pretty moment at the end of the ballroom scene. She had discovered the identity of the pilgrim and stood gazing after him as if entranced ; the Nurse took her hand to draw her away, and at once her attitude and gesture revealed a sudden inclination to assert her own will and character ; the entire submission she had always offered to her elders was a thing of the past ; she was entering a new world in which she would have to judge for herself. It was a subtle idea, very simply, but very effectively rendered, and thoughtful onlookers traced from it a development of the strength which marked the great refusal :

> Now by St. Peter's church and St. Peter too
> He shall not make me there a joyful bride.

The only fault found by the most fervent admirers of the American actress was the common fault of declaiming the potion scene, clutching at imaginary bones and shrieking at imaginary corpses. An actress qualified to play the part is surely endowed with sufficient facial expression to enable her to represent the terrors of approaching insensibility—at a period when anæsthetics were unknown—without recourse to anything in the neighbourhood of rant. The widely different judgment of the first-night critics and Lord Lytton, the latter reinforced by the opinion of all the later audiences, may be explained by the fact that Mary Anderson was not satisfied with herself on the first night ; she set to work to reconsider, and remodel, her rendering of the part, with the result that towards the end of the run, one Juliet would scarcely have recognized the other.

Rosalind was the one character in which Mrs. Kendal had " failed to attract " ; the poetry of course suffered nothing at her hands, but the boy's clothes sat uneasily on her. Since *As You Like It* was written, Rosalind may perhaps never have been played with the same spirit, the same sense, the same meaning—all melting into the same beauty—which Ada Rehan imparted to one of Shakespeare's most adorable characters. Never for a moment was the womanly charm weakened, yet it was thought that Ada Rehan rose to her highest point— higher even than as Katharina—with the denunciation of the Duke ; it was an overflow from a proud woman's heart which had for its reaction a burst of humour and madcap dare-devilry. For all who saw this splendid daughter of Ireland, and especially for those who saw her on a famous night at the Grand Theatre, Islington, with a whiff of Phelps floating about the neighbourhood, Rosalind and Ada Rehan will be perpetually associated.

At Stratford Mary Anderson was acclaimed as a perfect Rosalind, but the year of Queen Victoria's Golden Jubilee was to mark the chief emprise of her brief, but brilliant, stage career ; she would produce, once more at the Lyceum, *The Winter's Tale*, Forbes-Robertson should be her Leontes and she herself would " double " the parts of Hermione and Perdita. She confided to Tennyson her fear lest the bold attempt should be unfavourably reviewed, but the Bard warmly encouraged the idea ; it would be an admirable way, he agreed with her, of keeping alive an unbroken interest in the mother and child who are separated for nearly two whole acts, while it would happily emphasize the likeness between mother and daughter, a likeness certainly envisaged by Shakespeare in lines such as :

> . . . the majesty of the
> Creature in remembrance of the
> Mother . . .

There lies before me a letter in which Madame Novarro insists :

" My success was due to the same person playing the mother and daughter, for Perdita's resemblance to her mother is spoken of several times. I had Tennyson, G. F. Watts, and every one of the great lovers of Shakespeare to back me in doubling the part, and it is obvious that mother and daughter ought to look alike."

The " success " claimed was a rock fact ; *The Winter's Tale* [1] ran for 164 nights, by far the longest sequence the play ever enjoyed, and was only taken off because the lease of the theatre could not be extended.

[1] The failure of *The Winter's Tale* had necessitated the closing of Drury Lane in 1879.

Once more the critics were a little grudging in their notices, but the public, the all-important judge, packed the house for every performance and successive houses waxed more and more enthusiastic as the weeks passed on.

One tableau remains vividly in mind. Sarah Bernhardt, it may be remembered, departed from precedent at one point in the *Dame aux Camélias*. A minute before her death, Marguerite, buoyed up by the sight and touch of her lover, says : " *Je ne souffre plus, on dirait que la vie rentre en moi ; mais je vais vivre. Ah, que je me sens bien."* Instead of sinking back on a couch, and there expiring in the hitherto accepted manner, Sarah, to give emphasis to the suggestion of a sudden spasm of vitality, stood bolt upright, drew in a great breath as though in defiance of death, and then, as if cut down by a swift stroke, fell headlong to the ground, gaining as she fell, the most graceful and picturesque pose a dead woman could possibly assume.

No stage fall could exceed this in dramatic meaning, but even more effective was Mary Anderson's fall in *The Winter's Tale*. When Leontes defied the Oracle, she raised the great white veil she was wearing over her head, held it high with uplifted arms, while she seemed to be uttering a prayer, and then, very slowly dropping the veil over her face, she swayed and sank straight forward, though when prone the beautiful face was turned upwards. The fall was admittedly difficult and a little dangerous, and there was much surmise as to

" how it was done." It was no.conventional stage trick, and to minimize the risk of injury a very light spring mattress was laid on the appointed spot.

Looking back to many evenings spent at the Lyceum Theatre that autumn, one remembers how difficult it was to decide whether Mary Anderson were more admirable when she vindicated her virtue with all the dignity of an outraged queen and all the indignation of a slandered woman, or when she danced—there is no other word for it—through all the exquisite woodland scenes with all the grace and joyousness of girlhood. Certain it is that whether as a mother, or a child, or a marble statue, she presented a picture which no lapse of years could wipe from the memories of those who looked on it.

Two years later, in the little Roman Catholic church at Hampstead, Mary Anderson married Antonio de Novarro. Except when, during the War, she played Galatea with all her old grace, and, with beauty but little dimmed, the balcony scene in *Romeo and Juliet*, she never trod the boards of the stage again. One must not grudge her all the happiness of married life she so largely enjoyed, but she certainly deprived at least two generations of an artistic treat they would have richly relished.

Mary Anderson had retired from public view for many years when there stepped into the limelight a young—

very young—actress determined to show what eager and strenuous work could accomplish. Twenty-five years have passed since Gladys Cooper dawned on the public, lovely as a dream, but without displaying—except to the really close observer—any very marked dramatic ability. It was, however, quickly seen that a determined woman had decided that her beauty should be neither her passport to fame nor a clog in the steep ascent which she envisaged and in which there was to be no looking back and very little going aside to rest. It has been said that if an artist wished to draw with pencil a face entirely perfect in outline, he could find no better—perhaps in this country no other—model than Gladys Cooper. To a loveliness of face which is of a piece with lovability of character, she has harnessed unflagging energy and unflinching devotion to duty; she has shirked nothing and shrunk from nothing and has made every natural gift the pliant instrument of a resolute will. The light comedy rôles, the portrayal of heroines who have through all the play all the sympathy of the audience, are not the achievements which may hereafter assign to Gladys Cooper a front place in the gallery of actresses who have "won through." The deliberate choice of unsympathetic parts such as the wronged wife in *Cynara*, or the faithless wife in *The Sacred Flame*, or Mariella in *The Shining Hour* where the wind was in her teeth from beginning to end, prove her to be no fair-weather traveller on the path to popularity; rather is she an artist with

(*Photo by Dorothy Wilding*)

GLADYS COOPER

[*Facing p.* 118

sufficient grit to recognize that the greater the difficulty,
the more delightful it is to deal with it. And it is
perhaps because Gladys Cooper rates the work as far
more important than the workwoman that she is wholly
free from the slightest stain of jealousy. Watch her in
the scene in which " the other woman " or perhaps the
ingénue has the more effective opportunities ; she will
remain, as she would in real life, absorbed in what is
going on, but will, as far as possible, efface herself from
the notice of the audience. It is the whole stage, not
the centre of it, which is her consideration ; " The
play's the thing " is what seems to occupy every corner
of her mind every moment of her professional life.
Like all artists who have respected, as well as loved,
their profession, the theatre has been to Miss Cooper
the sum and centre of her interests and her intellectual
home. And like all good artists, like Sarah herself, she
is a *traqueuse*, whose forehead burns and whose hands are
icy on a first night, and who, with fever in the veins
and nerves strained to snapping-point, will yet perhaps
give the most inspired · performance of the whole run.

As yet Gladys Cooper has not nearly finished her
climb ; there are several important ridges which she
must still seize and occupy, and, at the time of writing,
two of them, Desdemona and Lady Macbeth, are her
objective. Desdemona will fall easily to her attack ; the
precise place which will hereafter be assigned to Gladys
Cooper in the gallery occupied by leading actresses may

depend on how far she makes good the challenge she offers, quite modestly but quite decidedly, to Giulia Ristori, Ellen Terry, and other women who, by common consent, hold the fort she is about to storm. New York is to be the base for her first attempt ; London will witness her later, and perhaps surer, attack

And truly no chapter on this subject, however incomplete and inadequate, can be closed without travelling back half a century, and a good deal more, to pay a tribute to Nellie Bromley,[1] the original, and devastatingly lovely, Plaintiff in *Trial by Jury*, and even to a famous figurante in Hetty Harmer ; the contribution of the latter to the stage was little else than to tread it, but she trod it with the carriage of a goddess, and her masses of auburn hair crowned a real complexion of cream and roses, as well as features which photographers strove in vain to reproduce.

[1] Mrs. Stuart Wortley, a friend of many years, is still with us and in excellent health.

CHAPTER X

BURLESQUE AND MUSICAL
COMEDY

"WHAT did you enjoy most in London?" was the
question put to the beautiful Madame de Gal-
liffet on her return to Paris after a brief visit here. "*Les
hansom cabs et Dorothy,*" was the reply. This was the first
of the new kind of musical plays destined soon to take the
place of the long-popular "burlesques" for which at that
time the old Gaiety Theatre was famous. And it was in
this amazingly successful piece—it played for a record of
931 consecutive performances—that Marie Tempest won
the earliest of those triumphs that were to set her at the
very head of the musical-comedy stage. Ten years later
she stepped gracefully from musical comedy to comedy
proper, just as, thirty years earlier, Mrs. Bancroft had
stepped from burlesque to comedy, and in each case to a
position without parallel within the English theatre.

There was another very famous lady who had thought
to form a similar intention. In 1891 Nellie Farren, that
"incarnation of chic" as she was called in the days when
she was "principal boy" at the Gaiety, announced to her

manager that she was playing in her last burlesque ; she proposed·to devote the rest of her career to legitimate comedy. The first part of her prophecy was fulfilled, but it was in tragedy rather than comedy that her future was destined to be spent. Within a month she was struck down by an illness that forced her into premature and permanent retirement. Her immense and widespread popularity was proved by a gigantic Benefit Performance, the arrangements for which were in the hands of a Committee which included three dukes, four earls, and the Lord Chief Justice of England.

The Benefit secured a large sum with which the Committee proposed to buy an annuity. The Rothschilds stepped in ; Nellie's span of life was not likely to be long and an annuity would be " giving it away " ; they banked the money, gave the tenant for life 10 per cent on it, and handed over the whole sum to her heirs at her death.

Dazzling Nellie Farren had for her partner bewitching Kate Vaughan. If Nellie was chic incarnate, Kate was *élégance* (there is no English word for it) itself. She was the first danseuse to wear long skirts, and their very swish exercised a special fascination ; her black silk stockings and black gloves set a fashion followed not only by well-gowned women but by ourselves. Night after night would there be seen three rows of serried stalls occupied by young men all wearing the black gloves that she wore and carrying the crutch stick she was supposed to admire.

A less talented actress tried to beat Kate Vaughan and appeared in black gloves with white thumbs, but her admirers were less ardent and no fashion was set.

The old burlesques were a very different type of " show " from the more refined musical comedies which eventually succeeded them. With their male impersonators, the jingling couplets and their fondness for puns, they were literally burlesque-versions of famous books and plays. There was a *Monte Cristo Junior*, a *Little Faust*, and an *Ariel*, the last-named being a travesty of *The Tempest*, which aroused protesting cries of " irreverence." They were a go-as-you-please kind of entertainment, which allowed plenty of opportunity for that topical satire which characterizes our contemporary revues. Occasionally this satire gave offence. Irving, for instance, persuaded the Lord Chamberlain to suppress a caricature of himself, his objection being, not to any cruelty in the satirical imitation itself, but to the indignity occasioned by the fact that the actor impersonating him was dressed as a ballet-girl !

Odd though it seems nowadays, Irving himself had acted at the Gaiety, as an almost unknown actor, in support of the famous low comedian, J. L. Toole,[1] and scored

[1] Apart from his personal friendship with Henry Irving, Edward VII said that the two actors who gave him the greatest pleasure to listen to were John Hare and J. L. Toole.

one of his earliest "hits." For famous though this theatre was for its burlesques, it was used between times for other purposes than mere frivolity. It was here, for instance, that Bernhardt and the Comédie Française Company paid their first visit to London. Réjane acted at the Gaiety, playing *Madame Sans Gene*, and unconsciously defying anybody else to play it like her. Phelps, with Forbes-Robertson supporting him, played Shakespeare there, and Swinburne contributed an "interpolated" song for the production. On one occasion even Mr. Gladstone paid a visit to the theatre, spending the whole evening "behind the scenes" and insisting on having all the stage mechanics and contrivances explained to him, and finally, as Hollingshead, the manager, recorded afterwards, "when he had collected enough material for a *Quarterly Review* article, he selected the best-looking young lady he could find in the Company and sat with her in the 'prompt-box' watching Charles Matthews act."

And it was at the old Gaiety, built by one of the proprietors of the "Daily Telegraph" and modelled on the Paris Théâtre Lyrique, that a partnership destined to give the world a new and unrivalled form of comic opera, was initiated when the first collaborated work of Gilbert and Sullivan, the now forgotten piece called *Thespis, or The Gods Grown Old*, was produced there. Gilbert, indeed, was represented in its very first programme, when Hollingshead, a former colleague of Charles Dickens in journalism, opened it in 1868, with Nellie Farren as his leading " boy " and Madge Robertson (later Mrs. Kendal) as his leading lady.

But it was as a house of " burlesque " that the old Gaiety was most famous—or notorious. For its frivolity was frowned on in the stricter sections of Society ; and when Hollingshead was proposed for the Reform Club, though his candidature was supported by the great John Bright, he was promptly blackballed by what nowadays we should designate the " kill-joy " element, chief among whom, according to the defeated candidate, was a gentleman who combined superlative respectability with the manufacture of pink silk tights, and of whose products, by peculiar irony, his victim had at the time six hundred pounds' worth in his theatre !

1894 saw the death of these old burlesques and the beginning of the more refined Musical Comedies, the first of which, *The Shop Girl*, ran for two years with a cast which included Seymour Hicks, George Grossmith and Teddie Payne. Daly's was added to the Gaiety as a regular home for this kind of entertainment, of which perhaps the most triumphant was *The Merry Widow*, in which Lily Elsie, who served to remind some of us of Florence St. John, leapt to the very pinnacle of fame. The vogue of these musical comedies and farces lasted till the War, when the revue, sometimes spectacular, sometimes " intimate," began to take its place as the favourite after-dinner show. Nearly contemporary with the birth of the revue was that of the " thriller." The progenitor of these may be said to have been *Bulldog Drummond*, the success of which induced Gerald Du Maurier to prophesy an era of " thick-ear " plays. In the revues, as also in the more legitimately musical plays to which one's eyes and ears are sufficiently often treated, the standard of acting and production, and not seldom of the plays themselves, has reached heights at which the managers of non-musical theatres may well have gazed enviously.

And one result of this has been that the process of theatrical migration has frequently been reversed. Instead, as happened with Marie Tempest, of the musical-comedy artist " rising " to the greater dignity of legitimate comedy, actors [1] and actresses who have proved themselves in " straight " plays, have been re-warded and their talents recognized by an offer to appear in revues and musical plays. No doubt the vastly higher salaries which this more popular form of entertainment can afford to pay, have been part of the temptation, but the fact remains that the modern artistic standards of musical plays are such that no actor could regard it as an indignity to appear in them

[1] Patrick Waddington and Derek Williams and even Lady Tree could be cited.

CHAPTER XI

THE STORM IN A TEACUP

IT was A. S. Walkley—whose services "The Times" newspaper enjoyed for so many years—who hazarded the opinion that, "without the Ibsen episode we could hardly have had the serious plays" of Pinero, Henry Arthur Jones, and their successors ; it might be more accurate to say that Ibsen hastened, and made easy, an inevitable renaissance, and that he himself was simply a sign, perhaps an early sign, of the times in which he wrote. His plays were the theatrical expression of " ideas " already at work in a world of which he knew little, and however revolutionary they seemed inside that lonely little microcosm called the theatre, they were in fact symptoms of a growing new philosophy of life.

The Norwegian dramatist has been alluded to as a germ-carrier, himself infected with the new rebellious spirit which refused to accept things as right merely because they followed inherited traditions ; the translation of his plays caused him to get close touch with the bolder English critics and the younger English playwrights, and these he infected with the itch to query every solemn prescription, hitherto meekly and obediently swallowed.

As a dramatic revolutionary Ibsen struck lucky; the '60's and '70's of the last century saw a drastic change in national life, domestic, social and political. The old aristocratic conception of society was rapidly slipping into our modern democracy and, while under the fiery leadership of Mr. Gladstone Whigs were becoming Liberals, Mr. Disraeli, with his shrewd eye fixed on facts, was busying himself to identify Conservatism with social reform and the interests of the working classes. Gladstone failed to carry the Reform Bill in 1866 ; Disraeli, a year later, sent a much stronger measure of enfranchisement up to the Lords where it was entirely smiled on, and all the while John Stuart Mill was pounding away with the doctrine of complete democracy and votes for every man and woman. Then, from out of the Crimean War there had arisen an heroic and romantic, but very sane and practical, figure ; Florence Nightingale, whether she knew it or not, was the herald of a general change in the hitherto accepted notion of women's place on this planet ; women's colleges were being founded and, at long last, their higher education was being provided for. Even the Church was affected by the spirit of the times and was taking notice of newly acquired knowledge and the claims, not necessarily antagonistic, of scientific thought. Darwin himself had stocked the booksellers six years before Tom Robertson's mild theatrical revolution,

fourteen years before Sir Edmund Gosse first called attention to the existence of Henrik Ibsen, and thirty years
before the first of his plays to be seen in England, *A Doll's
House*, was produced. To anyone unfamiliar with the
crusted conservatism which for so long marked our
English theatre, it might seem astonishing that we
needed Ibsen's influence to bring it into line with
the new philosophy rapidly permeating the world
outside its doors and quite certainly soon to knock at
its own.

Robertson's revolution had been of a purely theatrical
character. Tom Robertson, born only ten years later
than Queen Victoria, was essentially a Mid-, if not Early,
Victorian, and if he was the first to see the difference
between real people and the stock absurdities put up on
the stage to represent them, he saw it all with Mid-
Victorian eyes. Ibsen leapt up as an out-and-out revolutionary. Robertson, perhaps luckily for him, had been a
playwright first and a reformer a long way after ; with
Ibsen the play was a means, the end being the propaganda
of " new ideas." The inevitable result in a country
trained to look on the theatre as standing for the
amusement rather than the enlightenment of people,
was what Walkley wrote of as a " storm in a teacup."
The new, much trumpeted and even more vituperated,
" Drama of Ideas " was an alien here, and after a
brief and uncomfortable residence, slipped quietly
away.

Some of our native playwrights, however, had caught from Ibsen the spirit of criticism as well as his new technique which abolished soliloquy and the "aside," but their instinct was still to write attractive plays rather than depressing tracts. From Pinero to Priestley the writers who have catered for us have, in no instance, qualified as "highbrows"; as intelligent dramatists they have absorbed into their system the new ideas and have utilized them to give a flavour of criticism and occasionally a spice of moral unconventionality to dramas quite frankly written for the playgoer who is prepared to pay for his place, and enjoy himself in it.

"*Tout passe tout lasse*," and it cannot be easy for the young generation to understand why Mr. Bernard Shaw should have lashed himself into writing of Ibsenism as rendering the atmosphere of London "black with vituperation, with threats, with clamour for suppression and extinction." *Ghosts*, which many Ibsenites regard as Ibsen's masterpiece, provoked the loudest storm, and even the tolerant critic of the theatre was certain "that such a play could ever be produced before a mixed audience is, in this country, an utter impossibility." Of course the term "mixed audience" has lost its meaning. "*Mais, Madame, je n'ecris pas mes pieces pour les jeunes filles,*" said the younger Dumas to a lady who protested that her daughter could not see *La Dame aux Camélias*. To-day there is no play which anyhow the English demoiselle is forbidden to see, although there may occur passages in some of them which she finds it a little difficult to explain to her mother.

Between 1889 and 1897 a little procession of Ibsen dramas found its way into holes and corners of the English theatre ; their opportunity was chiefly at matinées before subscription audiences, and they owed much to William Archer who translated them, to J. T. Grein, who organized their production, to Bernard Shaw who recommended them to the readers of the " Saturday Review," and to Lewis Waller, who lent all his virile qualities and volume of beautiful voice to the interpretation of more than one or two characters. Martin Harvey, Lady Tree, Laurence Irving, Elizabeth Robins—the original Hedda Gabler— Sir Frank Benson, Genevieve Ward, were other exponents, while Miss Janet Achurch may remain as the actress who as Norah penetrated the furthest into the skin of Ibsen's heroines. Most of the performances were of a semi-private character and many of them due to the Independent Theatre, the English equivalent of Antoine's famous Theatre Libre. This plucky organization, which boasted more courage than cash, not only exploited English efforts to set up and prop up Ibsen but engineered the visit of Lugne-Poe with his company known as " L'Œuvre " for a week's performance, with cheap and shabby scenery, of his and Maeterlinck's [1] plays.

[1] " The Library of Pastor Rosmer," wrote Bernard Shaw, " got

Then there was the strange case of Mrs. Patrick Campbell. Miss Elizabeth Robins had arranged a series of non-commercial performances of *Little Eyolf* —the play which contains what was then regarded as the very "daring" speech, in which a wife reproaches her husband for his indifference to his marital privileges, with the words, " There stood your champagne ; but you tasted it not ! " For the very arduous part of the wife Miss Janet Achurch was engaged ; Mrs. Campbell, then at the height of her reputation, volunteering to play the small but extremely important and effective part of the rat-wife which she played superlatively well. A theatrical syndicate then decided there might be money in Ibsen done in what they thought the right way, and the play was to be run as a commercial speculation. But to waste a fashionable star on a minor rôle was, in their opinion, quite wrong, anyhow even economically ; Miss Achurch was given her notice, and Mrs. Campbell was promoted to the leading part. The change was a good deal less than happy. The star, especially if apt to be a little hazy about her lines, was not invariably a money-spinner, and the syndicate ruefully withdrew *Little Eyolf*

on my nerves a little. What on earth did he want, for instance, with ' Sell's World Press ' ? That he should have provided himself with a volume of my own dramatic works I thought right and natural enough, though when he took that particular volume down and opened it, I began to speculate rather uneasily on the chances of his presently becoming so absorbed as to forget all about his part ! "

132

after ten performances, the end being perhaps hastened
by a sad fact. Mrs. Allmers knew so little of her words
in the third act that she had to fetch the book and read
them from it.[1]

An Enemy of the People was given at the Haymarket
Theatre in 1893 and revived at His Majesty's twelve
years later, and it proved to be one of Tree's happiest
ventures. He may have shone more brilliantly in
Svengali ; he never shone quite so steadily as in Dr.
Stockman. " Our social system," said the doctor, " is
rooted in a lie." Tree was trying to kick up the roots all
the way, and one felt that the roots were by no means
getting the best of it. He poured forth his denunciations
of the pettiness and corruption in municipal life ; sometimes he carried the public meeting with him, sometimes
he infuriated them with the home truths he thrust home,
sometimes he reduced the assembly to silence by pelting
them with hard sayings, but all the time he carried his
audience across the footlights with him, and at the end of

[1] When Duse played Hedda Gabler in 1903 her memory for once
played her a sorry trick. But the critic who was always prone to
criticize her strayed a little into exaggeration when he wrote :
" While the Signora walked through her part, the prompter threw
himself into it with a will ; he worried everyone in the theatre
except the Signora herself who listened placidly to the prompter's
reading, and as soon as he had finished, reproduced it in her own
way. This process made the matinée rather a long one."

the great fourth act the audience were more breathless than he was himself.

For a past master of make-up like Tree, Stockman was of course child's play, but Tree gave to it the same care as if he had been playing in *Trilby*, *The Red Lamp*, *Beau Brummel*, or when doubling—a real *tour de force*—Mr. Micawber with Dan Peggotty. Tree's flair for make-up was truly remarkable, far exceeding that of any other actor ; he could alter the shape of his head as easily as he could rearrange his features, but unfortunately he could not remodel his hands, which were the weak part of his physique. Although the cares of production might cause him to be a little vague about his words on a first night, it was always evident that, word-perfect or not, he not only looked but really felt the character he was assuming. As Gringoire he felt hungry, as Svengali he felt musical, magnetic and dirty, as Fagin he felt himself an old Jew of the worst type, as Richard and John he felt himself a king.

By the beginning of this century several other " ideas," at one time so startling as to divide London into two great armies of fervent Ibsenites and infuriated anti-Ibsenites, were degenerating into truisms. The Ibsenite heroine had lost a little of her prestige. The New Woman had come to stay, although Miss Winifred

Emery's exquisite performance in Cazenove's play of that name gave her a momentary setback ; her independence and equality with men which at one time excited an angry outcry led by the Sovereign in person, has become an ordinary occurrence and the New Woman went far to justify herself when, fourteen years later, England had to speak with England's enemies without the gate.

But in justice to Henrik Ibsen let it be said that even if "Ibsenism" proved a storm in a teacup, without it we should have had to wait much longer for the genus of play which for the past forty years we have so keenly appreciated.

Arthur Pinero gave us our first taste of this fare in *The Squire* ; appetite came with eating and *The Profligate* was eagerly assimilated by a public beginning to move easily on the new lines. But not until 1893 did the dramatist boldly serve up for us his *pièce de résistance* with *The Second Mrs. Tanqueray.*

CHAPTER XII

PINERO

BEFORE the arrival of *Mrs. Tanqueray* Pinero's pen
had already been prolific. Half a dozen farces,
enriched by the unforgettable broad comedy of Mrs.
John Wood and refined by the quiet humour of
Arthur Cecil, had filled, generally to capacity, the Court
Theatre ; *Sweet Lavender*, with Edward Terry released
from Gaiety burlesque, had boasted a run beside which
The Two Roses paled and *The Wind and the Rain* is still a
fool. But in *The Profligate* he had trodden fresh ground,
and had tiptoed into what was then considered as the
unpleasant. True, Miss Ada Cavendish, an actress who
went so far towards fame that she ought to have gone
a good deal further, had impersonated Wilkie Collin's
New Magdalen, but the unhappy past of that " unfortunate " was kept well in the shadow. In *The Profligate*
irregular social intercourse was exposed, but held up to
bitter reproach by the virtuous heroine who opined that
her betrothed was no longer worthy of her. So uncertain, however, was the author as to whether " this sort
of thing " ought to be put on the stage at all that he

hesitated as to which of two ends he had written would be more palatable to the public.

It is no exaggeration to say that " Mrs. Tanqueray " startled London ; her advent gave a shock which reverberated through, and far beyond, the capital. For the first time an out-and-out cocotte, the " sort of lady " who could scarcely be alluded to in polite society, was the centre figure of a straight modern play. Whether it was due to the unexpected but undisputed histrionic qualities of Mrs. Patrick Campbell, an import from Adelphi melodrama, or to the sheer merits of Pinero's work, or to the audacity of his theme, may remain a question ; anyhow, all the world and his wife hurried to the St. James's Theatre which, however, was supposed to be forbidden terrain for the unmarried girl. " My daughter will be able to see this play next month," was the quite natural comment of the Duchess of Teck,[1] who witnessed the performance a few weeks before the Royal Marriage.

Autres temps, autres mœurs. What would be regarded now merely as an effective piece *à thèse*, a well-told story of a by no means remarkable episode, was alluded to as holding the spectator from first to last in the thrall of a horrible fascination. " Nothing more essentially hideous or squalid," thundered " The Times " newspaper, " has been set before the Theatre Libre or any of its offshoots."

The names of Paula Tanqueray and Mrs. Pat Campbell

[1] Mother of Queen Mary.

are indissoluble. An actress who had hitherto attracted the barest attention woke up on a May morning and found herself famous. For three hours Paula's petulance, her flightiness, her vanity, her irresponsibility, her total inability to reform herself, had fascinated a critical and quite unbiased audience ; for three months the realism of Mrs. Patrick Campbell, who actually blew her nose in the midst of her most emotional scene, was discussed at every dinner-table. So strong was Mrs. Campbell's " attack "—a quality of which some of her successors seem so sadly void—so hammered out every detail of the character as she conceived it, so worked up were her final scenes that it would seem to everyone, not excluding the author—that she had plumbed the depths of Paula's rather shallow nature. Yet a year or two later Norman Forbes-Robertson was to telegraph to his elder brother, " Madge has shown us a great deal more of Mrs. Tanqueray." The point Mrs. Kendal stressed was the mother-hunger of the woman who pitifully craved, and was willing to crave humbly, for the affection of her stepdaughter. She sought to hide the rackety life she had led, the hardened woman of the half-world was positively nervous in the presence of the girl straight from the convent ; she touched Eileen's hand, and when the hand was drawn away, there was bitter disappointment, not anger, in Paula's eyes ; she took up a little looking-glass to see if that sordid past was written on her face, and dropped it when she realized the gulf between

herself and the girl to whom, with the first pure impulse
she had known for years, she longed to be a mother.
With all this she added something which made even more
desperate than before the situation when she finds that
Eileen's husband is the man, much younger than herself,
for whom she once "kept house."

The climax, with rather more sexual detail, was found
again in Hervieux's *L'Autre Danger*, a play which the
Lord Chamberlain,[1] despite energetic protest, to which
the present writer was no stranger, would not allow
Madame Bartel to give in London; the refusal was the
more unfortunate because *L'Autre Danger* had been the
piece chosen when King Edward paid a State visit to the
Comédie in 1903. Imagination boggles at the thought
of the French authorities refusing to allow Miss Terry
or Mrs. Kendal to present a play which had been the
chief item in a Command Performance for the French
President.

There are reviewers of Mrs. Campbell's rather jerky
progress towards fame who affirm that Pinero's next
attempt, *The Notorious Mrs. Ebbsmith*, was the best thing
she ever did; anyhow, it proved to be something which
no one else could do. Owing to a contract with Tree
rigidly enforced, Mrs. Campbell had to retire from

---

[1] It is not to deprecate an invaluable institution to suggest that the
Censor has sometimes been a little over-fastidious. During both
periods of the insanity of George III, any performance of *King Lear*
was prohibited as being subversive of loyalty to the Throne.

John Hare's management at the Garrick Theatre in the middle of a run ; neither pains nor money were spared to find a substitute, but as *The Notorious Mrs. Ebbsmith*— (the half-starved platform-speaker's notoriety was rather limited) Miss Olga Nethersole, an actress of first-rate value and genuinely possessed of " *les larmes dans la voix*," was quite unable to keep up the pace set by Mrs. Pat. There are some, however, who will adduce the rat-wife as Mrs. Campbell's most telling effort, while one has heard sober-minded critics assert that, having seen Sarah, Duse and Mrs. Campbell in *Magda*, they preferred the rendering given by the Englishwoman. With William Shakespeare Mrs. Campbell has never been on quite easy terms, while pre-war playgoers who had only associated her with grief-stricken characters, were amazed to find, in *The Thirteenth Chair* and *The Matriarch*, that she possessed almost unlimited capabilities for comedy bordering on farce : whatever the future may have in store for her, her debt to Arthur Pinero will never be repudiated or overlooked.

With *Mrs. Tanqueray* Pinero had made a hole in a rather artificial dramatic fence ; with *Mrs. Ebbsmith, Iris, His House in Order* and *Letty*, he demolished the fence altogether. Illicit love, conjugal infidelity, actual adultery were the motives treated seriously, openly, but with no vestige of coarseness ; and in every case there was an underlying note of tragedy which served to win the indulgence of good people who roundly resented the

" suggestiveness " inherent in plays which had travelled across the Channel. Pinero had no use for suggestion ; in all his plays vice was never laughed at nor licensed, rather was it always squarely faced and severely dealt with. What he had to say he said outright, and thus robbed it of any veiled offence ;—in his mind's eye neither black nor white were ever grey.

Veiled offence was the charge laid to Mr. Mordaunt Shairp in *The Green Bay Tree* and to Mr. Priestley in *Dangerous Corner*. Whether on the stage there should be observed the Pauline injunction that it is a shame even to speak of those things which are done in secret may be a point for discussion. Racine certainly brushed it aside in *Phèdre* ; the Lord Chamberlain has adhered to it in forbidding *La Prisonnière* [1] although he was one of the first to recognize Bourdet's output as a tragedy without offensive word or gesture. In *The Green Bay Tree* and in *Dangerous Corner* the acting of Hugh Williams and William Fox was so delicate that, alike at the St. Martin's and the Lyric theatres it was up to the audience to take it or leave it whether " anything was really meant."

It was well said of Arthur Pinero that he could look into the heart of a woman, and thus the women to whom

[1] When Miss Isabel Jeans played Bourdet's *La Prisonnière* in London the author actually rewrote the ending to attune it to her new and as he said, " *plus vrai* " interpretation of his captive.

he has introduced us have been real to the core, more so even than the men on whom he did not seem to bestow quite so much study and care. He is not supposed to have drawn his characters with any particular actress in view, but he certainly fitted as a glove Winifred Emery and Irene Vanbrugh ; to the latter perhaps alone he imparted his innermost thoughts, and from her delicate work, whether as Nina or Letty, he sucked no small advantage. There are some now who are haunted by a line in *Letty* spoken in a whisper, but a whisper which penetrated the house. The *flaneur*, not too happily impersonated by H. B. Irving, had just given the girl to whom he was making ardent love, the belated information that he was a married man : " You might have mentioned it," was the gentle reply, spoken without a shadow of bitterness but with which Irene Vanbrugh contrived to convey a whole mountain of reproach.

Bancroft pronounced *Iris* to be " Pin's best work," though the old actor was not altogether satisfied with the original cast. Miss Fay Davies was a little too pale, Oscar Ashe perhaps a little too purple, and it remained for Gladys Cooper and Henry Ainley, twenty-five years later, to tune up the one part and tone down the other to entire general approval.

Close friendship has its perils as well as its perquisites, and in *The Big Drum* Pinero had not been able to resist a parody of some of his friend's pomposities, many of which were assumed and many more wholly apocryphal.

To the latter class may be relegated the fiction, widely accepted, of Bancroft paying a visit to Comyns Carr, then supposed to be on his deathbed, and murmuring in measured tones, "I have brought you some grapes, white grapes. I never bring black on these occasions." One wonders what is the masculine of *grande dame*; whatever it be, that character has no better representative on any stage than Allan Aynesworth. In *The Big Drum*, clad in strict mourning, returning from what a Society editor once described as "a smart funeral," with the melancholy reflection that there had been "no wreaths," Aynesworth gave a blend of Bancroft and a well-known individual who made a point of attending all important obsequies which almost, but not quite, enabled the dramatist to beat his drum to pecuniary profit.

To Pinero late in life also came a notion which had escaped contemporary playwrights; he would set Owen Nares a task in which the "looks" which had won a very light comedian so much feminine favour, would be entirely at a discount. As the war-maimed, twisted, mutilated cripple in *The Enchanted Cottage*, a popular actor was to prove, and prove unmistakably, what he could do with a part from which all varnish and polish had been scraped off. But facts as he saw them, not fantasies as Barrie wove them, were Pinero's stock-in-trade, and *The Enchanted Cottage* puzzled a good deal and paid very little.

To the author's admitted astonishment, *Trelawney of*

the Wells was the comedy, with unusually little stage carpentry in it, which seemed to grip public affection no less than public attention. This may have been because he was dealing with people and things within his own personal acquaintance ; he could write with heart as well as hand and brain ; he could enjoy himself in depicting lovable stage folk and in making them as extravagantly romantic as he pleased. Perhaps all unconsciously he was revealing his own innermost self, his love of the theatre and all that belonged to it, his kindly outlook on life which the bitter things he sometimes wrote did nothing to blur, his simplicity which no success could spoil.

His, very righteous, belief in himself forbade Pinero to accept any "outside" hints, and his characters sometimes said and did things which they would not have said and done in real life. One of his titled personages spoke of "purchasing my perfume," whereas "buying my scent" would have been a likelier expression. In *The Princess and the Butterfly*, the ·Princess of Panonia, an ultra-aristocratic, and presumably royalist, resident in Paris, gives a dinner and takes her patrician guests on to a party at the Elysée, a place in which, at that time, no member of a "French family" ever set foot.

The same curious reluctance to accept advice was manifest at a revival of *Fédora*. Sir George Buchanan, our Ambassador for many years in Russia, offered to attend a rehearsal and watch over little points which mark procedure in Russian Society ; the offer was courteously declined, and some solecisms, quite harmless but rather ridiculous, were the consequence. Even as regards the almost flawless *Journey's End*, the General Officer who had directed the Artillery in the War made a suggestion when he accompanied the present writer to the first public performance, which would have been even more helpful at a rehearsal.

As a dramatist Pinero in the flux of time may be remembered as an ardent admirer of Scribe and an intelligent disciple of Sardou rather than as an imitator of Ibsen. Take him at his best, there was much in some of his plays which any of these three magnates might have been pleased to employ. As a friend—well, most of those who knew him as such have fallen asleep, but in the thoughts of the few of us who remain, he has a corner all his own.

No knighthood of the drama, King Edward was sure, could be complete without Arthur Pinero being enrolled, and in due course he was summoned to an Investiture in the Palace. At the entrance to the Throne Room Beerbohm Tree, about to receive the same honour, whispered to the present writer, " Pinero is very nervous and wants to know if he can have gas." It required Tree's nimble brain to conjure up the accolade being bestowed while the recipient was under an anæsthetic.

CHAPTER XIII

OUR PLAYWRIGHTS OF TO-DAY

COMPARISONS are for the most part as unsatis-factory as compromises, and to compare great men with one another can generally be set down as an otiose exercise. How can one measure Mr. Disraeli with Mr. Baldwin, Mr. Gladstone with Mr. Lloyd George, the Duke of Marlborough with the Duke of Wellington, Sir Joshua Reynolds with Sir John Millais. Or, to penetrate into what has been alluded to as the " higherarchy " of the theatre, how can one set up David Garrick against John Gielgud, or Sheridan against Somerset Maugham? Foul fall the day when we suggest that the Men-of-the-Past were giants and the Men-of-the-Present pigmies by comparison. The Average Man, as he grows more mentally alert, creeps up intellectually nearer to those who are tasting fame, and he is consequently less and less impressed by their greatness. Criticism is abroad and doing something to rob us of our old sense of awe for celebrities ; up to a point we have become iconoclasts. In so far as the theatre is concerned it may be a little clumsy, but it is not inconvenient, to take the recent history of English drama by decades. Forty years ago Sir

Arthur Pinero was of course running very strong, and Sidney Grundy, Henry Arthur Jones and Oscar Wilde were well up in the race, although the last was about to be disqualified for other than literary reasons. Henry James, novelist and philosopher, had tripped up on the stage with *Guy Domville*, but Carton and the actor-playwright H. V. Esmond were not far behind, and Alfred Sutro had successfully collaborated with Arthur Bourchier in a farce adapted from the French called *The Chili Widow*. William Archer was moved to admit that 1895 was " a highly inspiriting year in the theatre."

Ten years later Sutro had come to stay, Barrie had given us a foretaste of what we were going to receive with what some people still consider his masterpiece, *The Admirable Crichton* ; at the " Court " too the Vedrenne-Granville Barker management were introducing the public to plays by Bernard Shaw, Galsworthy and Barker's own. Two years would elapse before *Lady Frederick*—put on as a stopgap and stopping the gap for nearly a twelvemonth—scored Somerset Maugham's first success, but the Stage Society, with fine flair, had given him his first chance with *A Man's Honour*.

Another ten years' jump and we are in mid-war. With the possible exception of *Mademoiselle Beulmans*, in which a Belgian company gave a timely hint of the horrors of invasion, and *The Man Who Stayed at Home*, the war play was postponed until long after the Cease Fire had sounded. The younger playwrights were engaged in acting, rather than in writing, drama ; the younger actors were hurrying to man the trenches. The audiences, in spite of the threat of air raids, packed the theatres but demanded certain sorts of entertainment, and if their demands were satisfied, phenomenally long runs were enjoyed.

1925.—New names now appeared on programmes and posters, though many had survived from the past. Bernard Shaw had gone from strength to strength. Barrie was conducting us, as he alone could, into realms of sheer delight, Galsworthy [1] was already occupying a pinnacle all his own, Maugham had proved himself as a brilliant writer of sometimes rather bitter comedies ; A. A. Milne and Ashley Dukes had added their names to the list of English dramatists ; Frederick Lonsdale and Noel Coward, the latter with all the daring of successful youth, were marching towards popularity and *réclame* ; Edgar Wallace was " thrilling " us and St. John Ervine, who could write with the same pen his own plays and his criticisms of other people's, was oscillating between stern

[1] I was at the first matinée of Galsworthy's *Strife*, which is worthy to rank with any *pièce à thèse* at the Comédie. The grim struggle between the head of the manufacturing firm and the leader of the strike is the most virile thing I have ever seen on the stage. It is war to the knife, and a fight to the death, for at the moment when the striker's speech at the meeting has reached its high fever-point, he hears that his wife has died of what is practically starvation. I don't know what—if any—moral is to be drawn, but the play is an eye-opener, and " The Times " is moved to say that the author has done much more than write a play, he has performed a public service.

(*Photo by Anthony*)

MARIE TEMPEST

[*Facing p.* 148

Jane Clegg and the light-hearted *First Mrs. Fraser*; the last might not have been quite so light-hearted without the effervescence of Marie Tempest and the perfect balance of Henry Ainley's Scotsman. Comedy and melodrama for the most part held the field. The problem play had almost disappeared, chiefly because the kind of problems which inspired them had themselves disappeared from daily life. "Society"—an odious word for which there is no equivalent—had become so mixed and so tolerant that no problem of moral or social conduct had sufficient importance or novelty to be capable of being treated seriously. People were very often bored but no longer shocked by anything, least of all by what had once been reproachfully regarded as unmentionable "secrets of the alcove"; one smiled at what had once been scandalous, and yawned at what not so long ago had been sensational. This new go-as-you-please of course deprived the theatre of that sort of sure-fire situation which had once been the mainstay of the West End theatre. Frederick Lonsdale did indeed contrive a post-war equivalent when he made the husband in *Spring-Cleaning* introduce a professional street-walker as the moral-pointing guest at a fashionable dinner-party; Maugham in *Our Betters* aimed less well at a similar effect when a wife was caught *flagrante delictu* in a summer-house by an innocent young girl.[1] Both these plays owed their vogue as much to witty dialogue and

---

[1] During the run of the play an alteration was made, and it was the girl's American fiancé who discovered her sister's infidelity.

blatantly immoral, or rather amoral, characters as to genuinely dramatic moments ; nor was it without significance that in Maugham's play the wife's infidelity was to her rich, elderly and vulgar lover, rather than to her husband, and that the happy ending was provided by her success in deluding this gullible paramour into a recon- ciliation satisfactory enough from a financial angle.

1935.—The autumn season, at time of writing, is still an undiscovered country. We have been promised new plays by Barrie and Lonsdale,[1] both of whom have been far too long absentees from the theatre. Malvern has been the birthplace of Shaw's pantechniconic disserta- tions and already he promises us another play with far more popular qualities. Maugham, brilliant and biting as ever, threatens that he has written his last play ; should this unhappily prove to be true he is inflicting on us a real and grievous loss ; he has given to the English theatre plays both interesting and enlivening and has endued them, as is not always the case, with correct local colour ; we cannot, we really cannot, afford to lose the man who is perhaps better equipped than any other tc write really " worth-while " comedies. True, that for once, or rather for twice, disappointment and he have walked together ; in *For Services Rendered* he had piled up agony on agony with a group of characters whose suffer- ings he—rather arbitrarily—attributed to the War. And

[1] Since writing the above, Mr. Lonsdale's play has been indefinitely postponed.

the trouble was, not merely that the whole thing was depressing almost beyond endurance, but that by 1932 all war discussion had come to be regarded as a weariness of the flesh ! But if here Maugham was dealing with a subject which had ceased to interest, in his next play *Sheppey* he did worse : he dealt with a subject which had ceased even to exist. There is evidence that *Sheppey* was planned when the writer was at the very outset of his career ; he pillories his characters not so much for their lack of ordinary generosity as for their failure to practise the Christianity they profess in matters such as loving your neighbour and distributing your goods among the poor. Unfortunately a large percentage of Mr. Maugham's audiences had ceased to be *pratiquants* and would barely admit themselves as *croyants*, so could scarcely be sneered at for refusing to obey the precepts of religion ; the whole argument of *Sheppey* was founded on a premise that had ceased to be true, and the play therefore fell through. Mr. Maugham is reported to have said openly that he is " no longer in touch with the public that patronizes the theatre " ; the obvious answer is that for the credit of the theatre and the enjoyment of the public, the sooner he gets in touch again—which should not be a very difficult matter—the better.

We have enjoyed in the years just behind us a very fair quota of good plays and a few of outstanding merit ; what we miss is established professional playwrights—men we can rely on for a regular and steady output whose names on a prospectus or programme assure at least good workmanship. Bernard Shaw, despite his seventy-nine winters, has no doubt a good many plays up his sleeve, but it is scarcely to him that the theatre, from a commercial point of view, looks for its supplies ; from Barrie we can scarcely now expect more than an occasional jewel, though it is sure to be a jewel perfectly cut and set and of the first water. Where are the reliables of thirty years ago, even if these were not of quite the same quality ? Frederick Lonsdale differs from the really reliable dramatist in one, by no means unimportant, respect ; he has not the same sheer irresistible urge to write which pins Bernard Shaw to his desk ; nor does he write as Maugham writes to-day and Pinero wrote yesterday as a matter of ordinary professional routine, the application of the methods of the business man to literature. Arthur Pinero would retire, regularly as clockwork, to his study after luncheon and there, guarded against all possibility of interruption, he would remain working often until midnight, a tray of food being passed into the room when rung for. Frederick Lonsdale frankly says that his interest in the theatre is shared with many others, especially politics ; half the joy of a success lies in the knowledge that he need not write another play for some time to come. He of course enjoys one advantage over Pinero and the earlier playwrights ; he can look to a very comfortable income from amateur and repertory productions [1] of a successful play and he can handle a lump sum, often of corpulent proportions, from film rights. As an offset to these large subsidiary earnings the shrinkage of profits from old touring rights must be reckoned with. In the provinces and suburbs the talkies have nearly ousted the acted drama, but still there stands the rock fact that a really successful play can provide a very enviable income, directly and indirectly, long after its original West End production. But if Lonsdale declines to conduct his play-writing on the lines observed by a medical practitioner, a lawyer, or a business man, the plays themselves are wrought with true professional workmanship.

This is as it should be. He served a long apprenticeship in the lighter forms of play-writing, though many, even of his friends and admirers, may have forgotten his large share in musical comedies such as *The King of Cadonia* and *The Maid of the Mountains* ; it was a post-war public to be first aware of Lonsdale as a writer of sparkling caustic dialogue. Like so many comedy writers he has two quite different styles and practises with them indifferently; he is no less happy in undiluted comedy (high farce might perhaps be a better name) than in comedy treatment of an essentially dramatic play. Just as Maugham has alternated between farces like *Home and Beauty* and plays like *Our Betters*, H. M. Harwood will joke with *The Man in*

[1] One well-known author, not quite in the first flight, is said to make between £4,000 and £5,000 a year from amateur rights alone.

Possession in the morning and treat seriously *A Grain of Mustard Seed* in the afternoon, so Lonsdale has contrasted sharply *Canaries Sometimes Sing* and *On Approval* with *The Last of Mrs. Cheyney* and *Spring-Cleaning*, both the latter being intended to convey a special meaning.

Harwood has listened to the call of Hollywood ; when will he, with his fine sense of the theatre, weary of the very lucrative but rather inglorious job of writing for the films ? Even more do we grudge America John Druten and any of his works. Younger than this century, his plays have shown little that is imitative, very much that is creative. He has brought a new and vivid interest into the theatre by finding drama among the most common-place classes of society and by refusing to turn them into " theatrical characters " he gives them to us just as he finds them ; he discovers their individual characteristic dramas instead of contriving drama round them. He has carried Realism a big step nearer to Reality ; one almost wonders whether it can be carried any further.

John Van Druten's very youth has enabled him to make young people his protagonists. This was vitally important in the second quarter of the twentieth century, when Youth was no longer snubbed and inarticulate, and Age—and even Middle Age—was finding itself forced to take a back seat. " Grown-ups should be seen and not heard " may some day be a rule of domestic life, although there are many of us to admit that one of the large compensations for old age lies in the thoughtful kindness one receives from young people. Anyhow, until the beginning of the century, younger people were subsidiary as dramatis personæ, they did little more than lend a touch of innocence or folly to a drama concerned almost exclusively with the affairs of middle age. And this was not only in accordance with the relative importance of the ages at that time ; it was also inevitably part-and-parcel of the actor-manager system. The important rôles had to be designed for men who had " arrived "—Alexander, Tree, Bourchier, Wyndham, Frederick Ker, and the like.

In the play which made Van Druten's name, *Young Woodley*, the title-rôle was a schoolboy ; in *Diversion* the principal male part was an unfledged youth. *After All* was a children's, rather than a parents', story ; and in *London Wall*, where the scene was laid in a solicitor's office (Van Druten had himself been apprenticed to the law), it was round the typists, junior clerks and office boys that the large interest circled.

Juvenile characters need juvenile actors. Or they should do so. But forty or fifty years ago, the boy-actor was unknown in our theatre, and a character like " Archie " in *A Scrap of Paper*, was played by John Hare, at that time a man of about forty—and a very poor job one of the most perfect painters of stage miniatures made of it !

Not long before his death Lucien Guitry said to me that the one thing lacking among French actors was *la jeunesse*. It was difficult, he complained, to get a really boyish performance, which he heard was quite frequent here. The reason, perhaps, is not far to seek. Military service, of course, cuts across the life of the young Frenchman, but also, as soon as he ceases to be an *écolier* he becomes a *petit jeune homme* and loses the freshness which the English boy retains through his twenties and which in the theatre is a valuable set-off for the greater technique which his contemporary across the Channel may boast.

The Lord Chamberlain hesitated as to giving his official sanction to *Young Woodley*. He may have remembered that Charles Dickens was loudly assailed by individuals who thought that they were being held up to obloquy as " Squeers," and he may have feared lest headmasters might call, or write, in angry protest against one of their profession being exposed to ridicule and reproach. More likely he thought that unless treated with the delicacy observed by Frank Lawton, Jack Hawkins and Kathleen O'Regan at the Arts Theatre Club, the theme might be disagreeable. Having been partially reassured on this point, his final and favourable decision was not uncoloured by the reminder that *Young Woodley* could not only claim to be a delightfully written story, but that it preached a very wholesome gospel : the bounden duty of parents to tell their children, before they send them away from home, the simple lessons of Nature. In one line, perhaps the key-line of the play, the father says : " I have never been very intimate with my boy " ; in other words, the motherless boy had been sent to school without any sex-knowledge, which was imparted to him in a most undesirable way by an elder, and rather coarse-minded, schoolfellow.

Another gospel wholly different but not less salutary, and to be taken to heart, was preached through *White Cargo*, a play in which Brian Aherne gave so exquisite a performance of young Langford that one grudges bitterly his capture by the New York theatres—where his Browning and his Mercutio were alike rapturously received—and the translation of his outstanding talents to that first cousin more than twice removed of the theatre, the cinema. In *White Cargo* there was taught the simple lesson, which so many of us overlook or forget, of all that is done and suffered by men who, year in year out, spend themselves, often with meagre reward, in the service of the Crown or of their employers, in sun-scorched outposts of the Empire, and who must sicken every day for the sights and sounds of home.

In *Diversion* Van Druten went one better than *Young Woodley*, though it was not nearly so good a box-office proposition. Cathleen Nesbit gave a perfect presentation of a cocotte who is bad simply because she has no sense of right and wrong, who is amoral rather than immoral. Maurice Evans was here to show us unmistakably the stuff of which he is made, and which has enabled him to give us at the Old Vic. a Hamlet and a

Richard II which few of his craft can be said to have
rivalled and which, in simple truth, scarcely one has sur-
passed. Certainly those who saw him here for the first
time were a little startled by his technique and there were
some of us to give rein to happy memories in recognizing
a voice of the same or nearly the same timbre as that with
which Forbes-Robertson used to hold us spellbound.

Incidentally the question was asked how he managed
the very skilful throttling of his inamorata; Bertlon, in
Fédora, solved the difficulty by putting one hand inside the
other, so that when he was apparently squeezing Sarah's
throat, he was really only pressing one hand against the
other, a " business " not devoid of danger if an excited
actor chooses the wrong spot for his " squeeze."

In 1932 Van Druten wrote a wholly adult play, *Behold
We Live*, and wrote it—as so many good, but not quite
satisfactory, plays have been written—" to order."
Here, instead of suitable artists being chosen for the
author's characters, the author created characters to suit
a couple of actors who could be relied on to " draw "
the public. The result was a quite interesting example
of the ordinary conventional drama, but, except in one or
two short scenes, there was very little characteristic of the
real Van Druten. Or it may have been that, with
Gerald Du Maurier and Gertrude Lawrence in the leading
rôles, Van Druten himself was submerged beneath two
powerful personalities.

Van Druten has given Youth a good many chances and Youth cannot be said to have missed any one of them. One does not expect, or even wish, him, as he himself ripens in years, to confine himself to juvenile characters. One would only ask him to go on painting directly from life, to choose his models from everyday, and workaday, folk and invest them with the same interest which other playwrights contrive around representatives of the leisured classes.

Mr. Priestley, whose delightful *Good Companions* suddenly hoisted him on to a pedestal well within public view, draws with no less accurate pencil than Van Druten though he may fill his brush with less attractive colours. Moreover, his *Laburnum Grove* goes to suggest that his work may hereafter be excepted from the rule that good novels seldom lend themselves to plays of the same worth. How many of us have revelled in reading, and re-reading, the *Villa Rose*, *The House of the Arrow*, *The Witness for the Defence*, *No Other Tiger* ; yet not one of Mr. A. E. W. Mason's stories came quite up to expectation when subjected to treatment on the stage. " Peggotty," Mr. Micawber, Oliver Twist, Colonel Newcome, Becky Sharp, were never quite so entirely human in the glare of the theatre as we found them in cold print.

The converse may be equally true. How few modern plays bear the test of quiet armchair reading ; indeed, if the armchair is specially comfortable, the perusal of the play may lead the reader to the land of Nod. We are not gripped as we were when facing the footlights. Was this a situation we thought so thrilling, or the epigram which set our shoulders shaking, or the speech which drew salt tears, of which we were no whit ashamed ? The fizz and the fun seemed to have evaporated ; the champagne has been decanted, and, if still quite agreeable, tastes a little flat. There is still to arise the novelist whose adaptation will " get across " ; there is still to arise the playwright whose play, whether in book form or not, will be read with the same zest that it is being listened to.

A word of sympathy cannot be withheld from the play-wright who has not yet arrived at the point of being able to dictate his own terms. The author of a successful novel has no difficulty in getting his second published, this being probably contracted for before he even begins to write it. But a playwright's position differs in one very important aspect from that of the novelist. A much-talked-about novel is inevitably engraved on the public mind with the name of the author ; in the case of a successful play, unless the author's name is already a household word, the play-going public associates it with the leading actors in it, and talks of having seen " Gladys Cooper's play " or of going to see " Ronnie Squire's new comedy." Indeed, the playwright's position was well summed up by Lonsdale in *Canaries Sometimes Sing* with the cynical phrase : " Only a third of the people who see his plays, know that *anyone* wrote it ! "

CHAPTER XIV

DICTION

THE same year which saw the creation of Mrs. Tanqueray in London by an artist who in it leapt to sudden fame, saw also the revival of *Berenice* in Paris ; the revival was due to the advocacy of Mounet Sully, the triumphant success to the art of Madame Bartet. It was a triumph, too, of mind over matter ; the Sociétaire, already nearly the doyenné of the Comédie, rose from a bed of sickness at the summons of the Directors ; tottered to the theatre for rehearsals, but gave on the first night, as thereafter for a hundred performances, a vigour and a sense of poetry to the part which drew the town again and again, and drew many of us from this side of the Channel to enjoy, and applaud, one of the greatest treats the Comédie has ever offered. Bartet was, rather than acted, Berenice, and she breathed such vitality into a drama that for years had lain on the dusty shelf of neglect that even when she and her companion Paul Mounet retired from the footlights and only Lambert remained of the old cast, Berenice still figured on the *affiches* of the theatre even if some of the audience shook their heads and murmured to their juniors : " *Ah, mais voue aurez vu Bartet !* "

" The theatre in my time," said Madame Bartet to the present writer only the other day, " was something of a religion, perhaps now there is not quite the same fervour and fever ; it is a question of how far the public can be amused and the artists make money. When Sarah left the Français all Paris received a shock ; while now a *démission* is no unusual occurrence ; Le Bargy, the incomparable Le Bargy, left long before his retirement was due in order that he might make and enjoy a fortune." But the delicious octogenarian was full of appreciation for the higher general level of acting which largely compensated for the eclipse of stars, and as she talked on in the cooing tones to which one had so often listened from " the front of the house," one remembered that it was to her Sarah pointed to find a model for diction pure and simple. Bartet's pronunciation, Sarah said, was not only faultless but infallible, and she would send any young friend who wished to study elocution to learn from one of these unrivalled exponents of it. Does one turn in vain here to find any artist who would serve as a model to our young actresses in this respect ? Why is it that no word from the lips of the Vanbrughs, Edith Evans, Ellis Jeffreys, Eva Moore, Dame May Whitty—and *a fortiori* Lady Tree and Miss Marie Tempest—escapes the ears of the pittite, while whole sentences of their very young sisters— with honourable exceptions, notably delightful Diana

Wynyard, Jill Esmond, Margharetta Scott *and* "Jean" —seem to be lost before they are midway across the stalls ? Happy the day when the English *ingénue*, so intelligent, so graceful in movement, so exquisitely—if exiguously—gowned, so perfectly shod and shingled, realizes that speech is handicapped, and held up, by a cigarette stuck in the corner of a rosy mouth.

Inaudibility, too often to be traced to carelessness, may in some cases be due to dental irregularities. A large jaw, for instance, gives an extra spurt to sound, while a deep palate imparts a sonorousness to utterances which a flat one denies ; a well-known tragic actress used always to put a little pink wax in the recesses of her lower jaw to obviate the " whistling " due to unusual width between her teeth.

A good prescription does not get stale with years and, mindful of her humble clients, Lady Bancroft's recommendation to her company to " plaster " the back wall of the gallery[1] still holds good ; the plastering, too, if properly prepared, should be as effective with a sigh as with a scream.

Personal reminiscences are apt to smack of anecdotage, but for sheer beauty Forbes-Robertson's delivery of Buckingham's farewell speech remains something of a

[1] " I have to think of the hearing and vision of the boy at the back of the gallery whose right to be put in full possession of the play is as sacred as that of the millionaire in the stalls or boxes."—Bernard Shaw.

sacred memory. The impression, night after night, left on the audience whose eyes were riveted on the actor as they drank in the intonations of his matchless voice, was that one of the noble army of martyrs had already crossed the dark river and was speaking from an unseen world.

A quarter of a century has passed since Johnston Forbes-Robertson—except for a momentary appearance in a family performance of *Twelfth Night*—has faced the public ; but for purity of tone and perfection of phrasing —no less than for excellence in his art—one has yet to look for his peer, and he has been at pains to say how much as regards diction he owed to a hint he received from the historian Brewer. " Extend your speaking register just as a singer extends his notes ; thus, and thus only, you will get not only flexibility but variety of tone."

Diction, we learn from an eighteenth-century writer, " consists in suiting one's words to one's ideas, and the stile to the subject " ; Ruskin resolved to put this theory into action by learning " absolute accuracy and precision of accent in prose." In vain does the dramatic author study the balance and rhythm of his phrases unless he meets with adequate response from the player in the matter of absolute " accuracy and precision " in pronouncing them.

SIR JOHNSTON FORBES-ROBERTSON

[*Facing p.* 164

CHAPTER XV

DISCIPLINE

"IT is only in England," murmured General Weygand to his A.D.C., as he drove away from the unveiling of Marshal Foch's statue, "that a military ceremonial can be carried out to perfection." The question is sometimes raised why the rehearsal of a military occasion always passes off with perfect smoothness, while the dress rehearsal of a play is generally disjointed and unpunctual, often chaotic, and occasionally seems to forbid the possibility of a first night on the morrow. To do the profession justice, the play generally is "all right on the night," but as a result of desperate eleventh-hour efforts. *Per contra*, the dress rehearsal of the Royal Tournament, or the Trooping of the Colour, or the Aldershot Tattoo, never call even for a moment's pause, and the same can even be said of a recent function when the King presented new standards to the Household Cavalry, although here a totally new ceremony had to be devised and drawn up, and the leading actor could not, of course, attend any of the rehearsals.

The answer is, of course, to be found in the discipline

to which the soldier instinctively submits himself and which makes him a pliant instrument in his superior officer's will. Discipline, according to good Sir John Murray, is " the training of subordinates to proper and orderly action, by instructing and exercising them in the same." Perhaps the chief difficulty of that sorely tried official, the producer, is to persuade some of the temperamental ladies and gentlemen committed to his charge that they are subordinates. This may be due to some extent to the disappearance of the actor-manager who, after all, had the double authority of an employer and of one who had reached the head of his profession as an actor, and was therefore a man to whom the other members of the company could willingly and naturally feel themselves subordinate. His mantle as producer has now fallen upon less distinguished shoulders, and a tactful co-operation between actors, author and producer has been substituted for supreme authority.

When he took over the Haymarket Theatre, Bancroft was asked why he did not continue a sort of club, which bore the title of the Court of No Conscience, in which the Haymarket Company used to divert themselves, during waits and intervals, with mock trials and debates, washed down as often as possible with a jorum of punch. The new proprietor laconically replied : " Because I don't approve of clubs in theatres. The actors are there to act and to work. They can amuse themselves afterwards when clear of the workshop." Mrs. John Wood went a step further ; during her tenancy of the Court Theatre no artist was allowed to receive any note or telegram until the final curtain fell. Kindly but firmly she would say, " I engage and pay for your services from eight to eleven, and during those hours nothing must be allowed to interrupt or traverse the attention, which should be absorbed in your work." With the solitary exception of Albert Edward, Prince of Wales, who always wished to pay his compliments to the leading artist, visits to dressing-rooms during intervals were always sternly discountenanced at such theatres as the Haymarket and the St. James's ; the artist was supposed to retain his or her stage character until the play was over.

On the other hand, it must be admitted that in Paris, where the theatre has always been taken seriously, visitors have often been encouraged to pay their respects behind the scenes during, rather than at the end of, a performance ; in the inner foyer of the Théâtre Français, Sociétaires and Pensionnaires would mix and converse with privileged members of the audience. But then in Paris, for some unknown but recognized reason, the play is not supposed to finish before midnight, the entr'actes are prodigiously long, and the artists generally have no false modesty about being interviewed when in the process of changing or making-up.

" Do you know So-and-So ? " said the great Russian *danseuse* at Monte Carlo to an Englishman, mentioning her partner. " Then come along and see him." A

knock at the door produced an immediate " *Entrez !* "
and the masculine ballet-dancer was found at his looking-
glass, without a stitch of clothing on his body. He was
quite unabashed, and without thinking it necessary to
make any excuse, entered at once into a lively and quite
unembarrassed conversation with his visitors.

On the other hand, a visitor behind the scenes at the
Criterion was scarcely less embarrassed than amused
by a well-known English actress, playing the rôle of a
French cocotte in some trivial farce, who had heard stories
of " Continental ways " ; hoping to impress her visitor,
she received him in her dressing-room with a similar
display of déshabille—a display made entirely ridiculous
by the Cockney accent blended with the broken English
in which, for some unknown reason, she saw fit to carry
on her share of the conversation !

" Would not So-and-so play the part all right ? " the
present writer asked Lady Tree. " No," was the reply ;
" So-and-So is not a sufficiently good artist to play a
small part." The remark was as pithy as it was profound. Very hard has died the idea that a part to be
effective must be lengthy, and that dignity is somehow
wrapped up in being on the stage and in the centre
of it, for as long as possible.

Give a really good player an inch of stuff, and without
over-action or undue emphasis, he or she will make it
into an ell ; give an indifferent player a long part, and

it will be reduced in all but a number of words into an insignificant inch.

Blanche Pierson, who trod in the footsteps of Madeleine Brohan at the Comédie, made one of the great successes of her eminently successful career when, during the War, she played in *Elevation*, although only about thirty lines fell to her to speak.

It happened that the present writer saw in Paris a play which, unless memory fails, George Alexander had bought. The first act was dominated by the mistress of the country house where the leading characters were among the guests, and during this act they completely subordinated themselves to the *va-et-vient* of the scene. The hostess had moments of delicious comedy, she was exquisitely courteous yet exquisitely fussy in doing her honours, and although through the play, which moved to a highly dramatic close, she appeared but little again, she had made an indelible mark on it. The famous manager of the St. James's Theatre was urged to engage the best and ripest actress available, no matter what the emoluments required. He willingly agreed at first to do this, but a series of unfortunate incidents led to the part being allotted to an artist who, however " capable," was of far from first-rate value. The first act fell quite flat, and only the gifts of a distinguished actor-manager, used to their very highest advantage, enabled the play to be received with fair favour. To-day the part of the hostess would be assigned to an actress of real distinction,

Madge Titteradge, Lilian Braithwaite, Violet and Irene Vanbrugh, Isabel Jeans, each of whom with every successive appearance, gives the lie direct to Ouida's dictum that if the autumn of life is often a man's apotheosis, it almost always spells the woman's *dégringolade*. There is not one of these ladies who is not far more "attractive" in the early-September, than she was in the mid-April, of life. Which of us who witnessed Lady Tree play irreproachably her rather pale parts in her early youth, thought that she would blossom into the richest autumnal *comédienne* since Mrs. John Wood ? Her chance came with Sydney Grundy's *Bunch of Violets*, and the Bunch of Violets was a *ballon d'essai* to atone triumphantly for the failure of Louis Parker's *Once Upon a Time* ; as a matter of history, it did not last much more than once upon a time at the Haymarket Theatre. Mrs. Tree had always been cast for the sympathetic, willowy, wistful heroine, and the question arose as to who should play the adventuress. "There you are," said Grundy, pointing a not particularly clean pipe at Mrs. Tree :—and there she was, and has been ever since, to remind us continually of how admirable a Zicka she would have been.

Whatever the relative value of the acting, unquestionably the " front of the house " in an English theatre is a

pleasant contrast with its equivalent in Paris. This is
largely due to the complete absence of a tipping system.
Those who grumble at having to pay sixpence for a
programme, the advertisements in which would seem
to have paid the cost of its production ten times over,
may take comfort from the fact that at least they do not
have to bargain with the sellers. The sum printed on
a French programme is simply the price (or so the gentleman who sells it tells you) that the programme-seller has
to pay for it, his livelihood depending on the profit-price
at which he can induce you to buy it from him. But not
even he is as troublesome as the often—to foreigners
unfamiliar with the custom—embarrassing *ouvreuses* who
expect to be tipped for having shown you to your seat,
or for any other human requirement that may arise, and
who do not hesitate to tell you, and everybody else in the
immediate neighbourhood, if they happen to regard your
pourboire as inadequate. Be it remembered that these
importunate employees have their justification in the
iniquitous system under which they not only receive no
remuneration but pay no small sum to be allowed to
officiate and extract what they can from their clients.
Well, too, may we comfort ourselves with the reflection
that strict regulations governing our English theatres
provide a more than sporting chance of escape should a
fire break out. Despite the warning offered by the
hideous tragedy of the Opéra Comique, the ordinary
French theatre seems a veritable death-trap ; in vain one

looks and longs for those " Emergency Exits " with which our English playhouses are so reassuringly provided.

The soldier who, a little scornfully, contrasts the dress rehearsals [1] in a West End theatre with the disciplinary methods and smooth working of a military rehearsal (which prevail in military amateur theatricals) must remember that whereas it is not for the soldier to " reason why," every actor in a play is to some extent a creative artist, his mind fully occupied, right up to the first night, with the thinking-out of ways in which, " off his own bat " and without too much coaching, he may perfect his own performance. And in some measure it may well be due to a wholesome lack of " discipline " by producers, and the consequent stimulus to individual intelligence and initiative, that the standard of small-part acting is so incomparably higher than it was when the actor-manager system was in swing. There is also the undoubted fact that the young recruits of the theatre spring to-day almost entirely from the more cultured classes, a happening so happy as to put into the shade

[1] The writer remembers going to a dress rehearsal of *Antony and Cleopatra* over forty years ago. Coghlan did not know ten consecutive lines of his part, and Mrs. Langtry, who had spent fabulous sums on her dresses and looked more beautiful than Cleopatra herself, was scarcely adequate. How Coghlan managed to get through—as he did —on the first night was a marvel.

the more commercial side of the question ; comparatively junior artists are so much more highly remunerated, that the "running-costs" prevent the moderately success-ful plays from being economically worth keeping on.

The payment of a salary during rehearsals to the minor actors, the soaring rents, the increased wages of the stagehands—all these and many other heavy costs have contributed to the necessity of speeding-up the produc-tion of a play. The scenery, the dresses, and the furnish-ings generally, have to be completed in the shortest possible time ; and this results in that last-minute rush and apparent confusion which always surprise and dismay the stranger at a dress rehearsal, yet out of which, by what seems a never-failing miracle, a smooth and hitchless first-night performance is evolved some twenty-four hours later. This means, of course, that the interval between the dress rehearsal and the first performance, far from being one of repose and recuperation, is usually a strenuous battle against time for everyone connected with the play.

Even to this day, in most London theatres, one sees a notice posted just inside the stage-door, forbidding visitors " behind the scenes " during the actual per-formance. Whether this rule is more obeyed in the observance or the breach, depends very largely on the individual management. But even where it is least strictly enforced, many artists refuse to see even their friends until the play is over. What is an interval devoted to leisurely gossip by the audience must often be the busiest ten minutes of the evening for the actor ; and the difference between French and English customs in this respect is greatly due to the difference between the brief minutes of an English interval and the seemingly unending entr'actes of the Paris theatres. Ten minutes does not allow too much time to reach a perhaps remote dressing-room, make a complete change of costume, and be ready for the call-boy's : " Second Act, beginners, please ! "

On first-nights a highly-strung actress is anyhow far too much of a *traqueuse* to have any inclination to exchange banalities with visitors until the final curtain has fallen. It may well be that, after the last dress rehearsal, last-minute changes or cuts are made, and these, however slight—and the slighter even the more trying to remember —are confusing to actors trained to the original version.[1]

The many difficulties peculiar to a first-night are probably added to, though of course with a compensating pleasure, by the " good-wish " telegrams and gifts of flowers which stream into the dressing-rooms of the principal players during the last hour before the curtain rises. A few of the telegrams will be opened, a few of the senders of the flowers identified by the cards attached

---

[1] Just recently, in Ivor Novello's comedy, *Full House*, one of the less important characters was removed altogether, and a new scene substituted, after the play had already been running for several nights at the Haymarket.

to them, but the rest must be left till the play is over, when the dressing-room is hastily prepared for the reception of friends, many of whom are persuaded that even for the leading actors a first-night is " great fun," whereas there have been three hours of gnawing anxiety, considerable nervous strain and sheer hard work.

No conscientious artists ever think of resting on their oars after the first-night, however crowned with success. Only after many performances will they feel confident of being word-perfect, and the dread of " drying-up " will have evaporated. There must be many like Isabel Jeans who rehearse to themselves every word of their part each evening before going on the stage. No two consecutive audiences are quite alike in the way they " receive " a play, and the artists really sensitive to the way a scene is " going " will adapt their playing to the mood of the audience.

Perhaps in England there is little of that gradual change in the general character of the " house " to which Sacha Guitry has lately drawn attention in respect of Parisian audiences ; he bluntly says that after the hundredth performance of a comedy he deliberately broadens the whole style of presentation, and again after the two-hundredth, so that, in the last state, what was originally a comedy becomes a farce. A British audience varies from night to night ; for some obscure reason its temper is said to be dull and unreceptive on Mondays, as to be specially appreciative and ready with applause at the end of the week.

Conscientiousness was carried to its limits the other day by an actor cast to play the Usher in a law-court scene. His microscopic part consisted of the one word "Silence!" which he had to call out on two or three occasions to give verisimilitude to the proceedings, and the "business" of handing a glass of water to the heroine when, under the stress of cross-examination by a ruthless Counsel, she was near collapse. After one rehearsal the author, on leaving the theatre, noticed one of the typescript "parts" lying in the gutter of the street outside. Picking it up, he discovered that it was the Usher's part, either dropped by accident or flung down in disgust, he was never quite sure which! But on opening it, he was astonished to find, written all over the margins of the two typed pages, manuscript notes, scribbled by the actor, of realistic "business" he had thought out to embellish his performance. This admirable intention did not come off when, on a particularly warm afternoon, the heroine arrived at her collapse and the moment came for the glass of water to revive her; the Usher was fast asleep, and the strange and unseemly spectacle was seen of the ruthless Counsel leaving his seat and doing the Usher's business for him! Later, when reproved for his somnolence, the actor blandly explained that during rehearsals he had spent much time at the Law Courts, studying the ways of real ushers;

that he had observed their habit of dozing, and that the trouble had occurred simply because he had deemed it artistically right to imitate this forensic habit, and the warmth of the afternoon had turned his conscientious simulation into momentary reality!

CHAPTER XVI

SARAH: THE LAST PHASE

"*JE vous en prie,* My Lord, *donnez-moi l'autorisation de partir par Boulogne. Le voyage par le Havre est une véritable torture. Je sais que ce que je demande est très difficile ; mais je sais aussi que cela est possible si votre grâce le veut bien.*

"*Quand même,* My Lord, *je vous serais très reconnaissante pour l'effort que vous voudrez bien faire.*

"SARAH BERNHARDT,

"Savoy Hotel."

So ran the letter—itself so highly perfumed as to cause some consternation in the corridors of the War Office—addressed by Madame Sarah Bernhardt to Lord Kitchener. The private secretary was at once commissioned to tell the veteran actress that if she persisted in her wish official permission would be forthcoming, but a corollary was added to the message, to the effect that the Folkestone-Boulogne route was then very hazardous, as enemy craft were busy in the Channel. For all answer, Sarah said : "*Mais alors c'est une question de mourir avec les soldats. Quelle gloire !*"

178

Sarah had been in London for an engagement at the Coliseum, which was crowded night after night to hear her recite her part in Eugene Morande's dramatic poem *Les Cathédrales*. Here she was seated, or rather enthroned, as Strasbourg Cathedral, on a pedestal far back on the east stage. She remained almost motionless; a slight uplifting of the hands was the only gesture; but there was all the old vehemence of utterance, all the perfection of phrasing, the outbursts of passion, the tears in the voice. "*Pleure, pleure, Allemagne; l'aigle Allemand est tombé dans le Rhin*," was the refrain, and the ringing tones rang true in prophecy, though then it was France who was weeping in her misery while Germany was exulting in her infamy.

Les Cathédrales gave way to a one-act piece, *Du Théâtre au Champ d'Honneur*, written by a French officer, and founded on a real episode which occurred on the French front. Sarah played—a veritable *tour de force*—the part of the young soldier who had been an actor, and from whose lips his comrades are never tired of hearing the *Prayer for our Enemies*, a poem which supplicated the Divine Judge to mete out just punishment to those who had stretched Belgium on the rack, had violated women and murdered helpless children. When the curtain rose, Marc Bertrand, a young French soldier, is lying on the ground, slowly regaining consciousness. It is the early morning, and during the previous day the Germans had fought furiously for the possession of the wood hard by. The boy is badly wounded, but all his thoughts are for the flag which he was clutching when he was shot down. How did it happen? Slowly it comes back to him that his colonel and his comrade were killed, and that soon afterwards his own father, proudly bearing the regimental colour, fell also. A German had sprung forward, but only to find Bertrand standing ready to defend the flag and avenge his father's death. The German was thrust back, mortally wounded, and Bertrand recovered the flag. He remembers this, but no more. At the sound of footsteps he grasps his revolver, but it is an English officer who comes forward and offers the parched and bleeding boy his water-bottle. He has heard of the young Frenchman who has come from the stage to the trenches, and has heard also of the prayer, which he asks him to repeat. The boy begins:

> " *Vous qui recompensez, dit-on, le sacrifice,*
> *Vous qui savez peser et juger l'idéal*
> *Dont un peuple se fait le lige et le féal*
> *Vous qui ne voulez pas que l'innocent patisse,*
> *Vous devant qui l'orgueil du mal n'est pas permis,*
> *Lorsque pour nous ainsi que pour nos ennemis*
> *Nous entendons sonner l'heure de la justice,*
> *Vous qui voyez, Seigneur, leur âme jusqu'au fond,*
> *Ne leur pardonnez pas . . . ils savent ce qu'ils font.*

> *Ils ont souillé de sang les pages de l'histoire ;*
> *Trahissant les serments, déchirant les traités.*
> *Ils ont fait reculer d'un bond l'humanité*
> *Jusqu'au seuil oublié des heures les plus noires,*
> *Et lorsque devant eux, en un sublime effort,*

Un peuple au déshonneur a preferé la mort,
Ils l'ont crucifié sans frémir, dans sa gloire.
Vous qui voyez, Seigneur, leur âme jusqu'au fond,
Ne leur pardonnez pas, ils savent ce qu'ils font."

In the latter stanza, Sarah's voice seemed to have regained not only all its former beauty but, by what must have been a great effort, all its former vibrant force. From the second line the voice rose higher and higher, to halt and break down into a sob on the " *un peuple a preferé la mort,*" and in the last line, when voicing France's prayer for vengeance, the tones became a rapid staccato, with a biting accent on the initial consonants, and the " they know what they do," was hurled out in frenzied insistence. In the last stanza the voice sank as if overcome by weakness, but every syllable cut across he house :

" *Abreuvez-les de pleurs. Faites que rien n'efface*
L'horreur du crime dont palpite l'univers ;
Doublez pour eux les maux dont nous avons souffert,
Frappez-les, O Seigneur, d'une main jamais lasse,
Jusqu'au jour où, pour délivrer l'humanité
Votre juste vengeance, en sa sure equité,
Du monde pour jamais abolira leur race !
Vous qui voyez, Seigneur, leur âme jusqu'au fond,
Ne leur pardonnez pas, ils savent ce qu'ils font."

The Englishman is awestruck by the agony of the prayer, and sees that Bertrand is growing weaker. A dog belonging to the Red Cross Society comes up, and the soldier gives him his blood-stained handkerchief and cap to carry to the nearest ambulance. Soon the stretcher-bearers arrive, but Bertrand refuses to leave without his flag. He is dying fast now, but in a flash he remembers that he hid it in the trunk of a tree close by; the tattered colour is brought, his fingers clutch it, and he can now die with honour. With a last effort he raises himself to hold it up, murmuring Déroulède's lines:

> " *Porte-drapeau, mon camarade!*
> *Au combat comme à la parade*
> *Ton chemin est le droit chemin.*
> *C'est un fier poste que ton grade!*
> *Porte-drapeau, mon camarade,*
> *Tu tiens la France dans ta main.*"

It is all over; the young soldier-actor has played his last part; the British officer uncovers: " *Vive l'Angle-terre!*" " *Vive la France!*"

" *Ne leur pardonnez pas,*" a terrible cry—more terrible even than Réjane's *Carillon*; a terrible appeal to Eternal Justice, and from Sarah's lips it seemed as if the very soul of a people were athirst for vengeance. And then with the recovery of the emblem of France the cry for vengeance changed into a cry of ecstasy, and, finally, with the whispered "*La France*" ecstasy died down into peace. Victory was sure and Eternal Wisdom would judge.

" *Altesse Royale, je mourrai en scène; c'est mon champ de bataille.*"

It was a hot July evening in London. Sarah had rehearsed all the morning, she had played *La Tosca* in the afternoon, and at night had given by special request *Fédora* in the presence of the Duchess of Teck, that devotee of the theatre, before whom all artists delighted to act. At the end of the performance the Princess talked long with the actress; she could tell her of Mademoiselle Rachel at Windsor Castle, she herself had also seen Rachel play Adrienne Le Couvreur, and had thought the great tragedienne very wonderful, but curiously lacking in charm; she could tell her—which pleased Sarah greatly—that Queen Victoria had spoken with enthusiasm of the command performance at Nice, and with regret of having so long postponed the pleasure of seeing her—and then in graceful phrase the Princess asked if Madame Sarah were not worn out after such a day's work.

" *Altesse Royale*," was the answer, with head thrown back, and in accents which bore no trace of fatigue, " *je mourrai en scène; c'est mon champ de bataille.*"

And surely it would have been her choice that death should come to her without wait or warning, as in the long past days she thought it would have come in *Zaire* [1]

[1] Sarah was compelled by the Directors to play Zaire on a sultry August evening when she was feeling ill. She was sure she would die during a very strenuous performance, as had once actually happened to an actor in the play. She strained every nerve, she sobbed, she suffered, and at one moment actually thought herself *in extremis*. But to her great surprise, when the final curtain fell she

—come in all the fullness of her fame and in the place where she reigned supreme. "*Un beau soir mourrez sur la scène dans un grand cri tragique,*" Jules Lemaître said to her when the laurels were just beginning to cluster on her brow. "*Mourir en scène*"—the words were often on her lips, and they were not to be very far short of fulfilment.

In the summer of 1922, Lucien Guitry asked Sarah if she would play with him in the *Sujet de Roman*, the four-act piece which his son had just completed. She would have none of the fatigue of production, physical difficulties were not prohibitive, she would remain seated during the whole act in which she was dominant, there would be no great demand on her emotional, and none on her declamatory, powers, but all the grace of her exquisitely feminine art would be in high relief. Sarah accepted with delight; it was delightful in itself to gather up the threads of comradeship with Guitry; the part pleased her greatly; that it was a part of secondary importance did not weigh a straw in her calculations. Everything went well; the miniature theatre lent itself to the delicate story; success was sure; the *Première*

had never felt better in her life, and the occasion always served to remind her that her vitality was a talent with which she could freely trade, that lassitude would find no lodgement in her body, as no failure would in her thoughts.

was for the 19th of December with the *Répétition Générale* on the previous evening. All the afternoon of the 18th Sarah had spent in the theatre, and she preferred to remain quietly there while the others went to dine before the *Répétition*. Then, in M. Sacha Guitry's luxurious room, which he had arranged for her use, just an hour before the three knocks should have been given, came the swift, sharp stroke which, in a moment, laid her low. Doctors were hurriedly summoned ; the news spread like wildfire that Sarah was suddenly and grievously ill ; journalists trooped in to try and learn exactly what had happened ; the *Répétition* was cancelled, and the *Première* indefinitely postponed. But stage curtains might rise and fall, Sarah would never again be found behind them.

CHAPTER XVII

WAR PLAYS

AT the beginning of 1909, just when Paris was mourning the death of Coquelin, London was flocking to Wyndham's Theatre to see *The Englishman's Home*, for which Gerald Du Maurier's equally clever soldier brother was responsible. The moral of the play, stripped of its rather crude business, was that the Englishman, believing himself perfectly secure in his island home, would not realize the danger which modern conditions carry, and regarded it as a great hardship to take any part, other than he chooses himself, in defending his country. This point had topical weight for a great territorial magnate had just refused leave for troops to traverse his grounds in the course of autumn manœuvres. In *The Englishman's Home* there were a good many tirades about our military shortcomings, our lack of military man-power, the ignorance of the auxiliary forces, the incompetence of their officers, the pooh-poohing of any idea of reform or of general service as then advocated by Lord Roberts.

And then, in this typical middle-class British home-

stead, the rather got-up grotesque was suddenly turned
into the grim. Two foreign officers appear in the door-
way demanding a surrender, there is a whistle of bullets
outside, the Cockney youth is shot through the heart
as he is perpetrating a Cockney joke, the John Bull
owner of the home snatches up a rifle which he does not
know how to handle, shoots one of the invaders and is
himself summarily executed as a civilian bearing arms.
Then as the daughter wailed over her father's corpse
there was the sound of bagpipes, the British Army was
being brought up by train and bus to the vulnerable spot,
and the invaders were caught in a trap. It all seemed
rather farcical and very far-fetched, yet a well-known
soldier was moved by it to write :

" I don't suppose this is really any great exaggeration
of our general inability to understand how entirely
topsyturvy and inside out our situation would be if,
at any time, our ' thin red line of heroes ' were too thin
to keep out, and keep off, a powerful enemy."

Nor perhaps would the author, himself to fall finely
in the War, think he had been so very far from the mark
if he could have heard Kitchener exclaim five years
later : " Did they remember when they went headlong
into a war like this that they were without an army or
without any means to equip one ? "

For only five years were to elapse before, in a back
street in Bosnia, a frenzied patriot fired a pistol ; within

five weeks five white nations were standing at arms and easy-going, peace-loving England must be transformed by swift master-strokes into the dominant military Power.

And with a few, a very few, lamentable exceptions, no stouter, keener, more efficient, more eager recruits were found than were gathered from *the* profession. The "boys" sprang to arms, the men "past age" pleaded to be allowed to do something for old England ; that "something" might mean long hours spent in hospital wards cheering men maimed and mutilated from the firing-line, it might mean strenuous hours in Q work on either side of the Channel, it might mean "something" which led to No-Man's Land. One veteran comedian of over sixty years got himself, by some means or other, enlisted in the R.A.M.C. and was found doing duty at an advanced dressing station. There were many whose names had figured on theatrical programmes to earn high distinction ; none, except those who remained aloof while their country was agonizing, to incur a shadow of reproach ; there were many hurt, some beyond repair ; there were many to go forward and overcome the sharpness of death. Truly, when England spoke with a fierce enemy there were no braver men to face that enemy than those who had hitherto only been called on to face the footlights.

When, in November 1918, the Cease Fire sounded, it seemed that a maimed and scarred generation might shrink from books or plays dealing with a tempest of fire and blood ; the wounds were still bleeding, and for thousands upon thousands all the glory of victory was only seen through a mist of tears. But in the flux of time there became apparent a feeling that it was not wise to fold away the memories of a fight into which England had flung herself because her honour was at stake ; some of the lessons of the War must be taught to those who had been too young or too old to learn them at first hand, and Philip Gibbs, Ian Hay, Wilfred Ewart, Mottram, Ernest Raymond and others began to be busy with narratives in which the honours and the humours of war were set out in high relief.

But the War—to which Douglas Haig set a term eight months before the date prescribed by Downing Street—had been over for more than four years before the Repertory Players set the example of using the long-drawn-out story of blood and agony as a peg on which to hang a drama. *Havoc* was the title of the play and, true to history, the havoc wrought was not only due to the German guns ; here, however, it was a woman in the case. Violet Derring, a second-rate, but much-advertised, beauty in a third-rate section of society was engaged to a Company Commander, Roddy Dunton, but fell in love with one of his subordinates, Dick Chappell, when home on leave. She sent the Lieutenant back to the front with the engagement ring, and the Captain, impersonated with a full measure of truculence by Leslie

Faber, furious at being supplanted in a woman's affections, ordered the young officer to take up an advanced post intending to abandon him to certain death. With the third act came a harrowing scene when a still younger subaltern, known as the Babe, and who had hitherto made a joke of the whole thing, was brought in half demented by the horrors of desperate hand-to-hand fighting in which he had shared for the first time. Rushing at Roddy, the boy accused him of deliberately withholding an order, which had come through, to withdraw from the redoubt and of leaving its tenants a prey to the enemy. Dick, however, made a surprise appearance ; he was maimed and blinded, but he and some of his platoon had made their escape, the escape which ensured a court-martial for Roddy who, with a redeeming gesture of remorse, blew out his brains.

Dick returns to England bent on offering Violet her freedom, but the wanton was to forestall him ; in a freezing note of dismissal she let him know that there was no place in her life for so hopeless a victim of German hate.

In a series of moving pictures, one Mr. Harry Wall painted, without any trace of exaggeration, some of the grim realities of happenings in France and Flanders ; no less certainly, if incidentally, did he remind us that the Kaiser's men of war were not the only malevolents whom soldiers—from the Commander-in-Chief downwards—were at times called upon to deal with. One little scene exquisitely, because so simply, played would by itself have prevented the play from being valueless. Henry Kendall's cheerful forecast of all he would be able to do, despite his blindness, was a wholesome reminder of the debt the country owes to men who with equal pluck and patience bear the loss of the most precious human asset, the eyesight of which the German bullets robbed them. "A temporary inconvenience, I assure you, my Lord," said one of the denizens of St. Dunstan's to the Bishop of London, declining any commiseration even before it was offered.

The Haymarket Theatre quickly made a bid for *Havoc*, and the sensation of their first night was the reception given to a then comparatively unknown actor, Richard Bird. So powerful, and so painful, was the outburst of the overwrought boy that the curtain rose thirty-five times for him to receive the tribute which a startled West End audience paid him. Sir William Robertson, the only English soldier to rise from the ranks and grasp a Field Marshal's baton, congratulated the young actor both on his performance and his war service. Said Bird, "I must tell you, sir, I never got my commission." "No more did I for ten years, so that means nothing," was Wully's characteristically blunt reply.

Havoc led a long line of plays concerned with the theatres of war, some coloured by romance, some akin to allegory, one—and one of the best—illustrating the deadly, and demoralizing, dullness of interment in

Switzerland. *Prisoners of War* dealt with abnormal conditions, and more than one of the Prisoners became a good deal other than normal ; rather thin ice had to be skated over, and it remained for Robert Harris to negotiate some difficult passages so carefully and skilfully as to render it ambiguous whether even any " veiled offence " were implied.

Le Tombeau sous l'Arc de Triomphe met at the outset with an ugly demonstration at the Comédie, not because of any disrespect to France or her valiant army, but rather because of the suggestion that a father had usurped the place of his son alike in his possessions and in the affections of the son's fiancée. It was an offence against the sense of *autorité paternelle* still strong in France, although here it had given way to a healthy mutual confidence between father and son which the emancipation of youth has done much to bring about ; the young warrior's bitterness in the last act was due to its being borne in on him that his father had been unfaithful to a trust ; the lands, no less than the love of the girl, belonged to the son, and his sire had encroached, without perceiving the injustice, on both. The only objection raised to the *Unknown Warrior* (Cecil Russell's clever adaptation of the *Tombeau*) in this country was the title which was supposed to be sacred to the soldier who sleeps within the walls of the great Abbey Church. The scene which gave the electric shock to the audience was when the Soldier addresses the shadows of the comrades who had lived and laughed and marched and fought alongside of him, and who were lying, stiff and cold, somewhere between the Sea and the Somme. There were some to murmur that this outburst did something to traverse the reality of the rest of the play set in one of those modest French country houses which yet bear the label of château. The larger opinion was that the greeting to the friends who had gone ahead and whom he was so soon to join only deepened the tragedy of the boy's brief, and interrupted, homecoming. Dame Madge Kendal was so impressed with the beauty of the Soldier's appeal that she said the curtain ought to have fallen on it; what followed in the act, however brief, came as an anticlimax.

The young soldier's betrothed had believed herself to be deeply, irretrievably in love with him before the War began, she was sure that every day of his absence would be an agony to her, but as the weeks and months went by she found herself more and more able to carry on without him, more and more content with doing the duties of the *ménage*, more and more at home with the older man in whose affections she had begun to lodge. She realized that her love for the Soldier had paled into liking, and liking had faded into indifference. She hugged herself with the idea that the war would soon be over and that with marriage the old feelings would revive, sufficiently anyhow, to prevent his finding out that they had never lapsed. And then the Soldier comes back on the short leave which he had bought at the price of leading a forlorn hope on his return, and the girl knows that, although she is willing to yield herself to him for the one night they are under the same roof, her old love for him is cold and dead. She tries to conceal this but in vain, and to the Soldier it is the summing up of all the mud and misery of the War, a foretaste of the death which he knows almost certainly awaits him.

The part of Aube, the girl, was played by Miss Jessica Tandy with a delicacy for which no praise could be too high, and Henry Ainley, among other experts, was forward to urge that the childishness of her appearance, the sense that she had not crossed the threshold of womanhood, deprived the night of love of the slightest suspicion of grossness. The story was one that required youth to portray it, and Maurice Evans's youth [1] made the despairing cry, " I don't want to be a hero, I want to come back," the more poignant ; the boy must have felt how unspeakably hard it was to break off life when life was only just beginning. And he goes back as so many boys went back, with a smile on his lips and with the icy conviction in his heart that death is waiting round the corner ; and here with the added pain that there would

[1] Maurice Browne played the part originally, and with considerable ability, but the essential quality of youth was lacking.

be no one at home to look and long for him, no one to feel that the empty place every day grew emptier.

Whatever its dramatic merits, the *Unknown Warrior* was much more than a war play, it was a mournful gospel to teach one of the saddest lessons of the War.

Suspense, to cite another of a quartette which cling closely to mind, was in a sense a modest pendant to the more famous *Journey's End.* Mr. Robert Sheriff dealt with first-hand knowledge of officers in the great German push of 1918 ; Mr. Patrick McGill, having served with honour in the ranks of the Royal Irish, knew precisely what he was writing about when he told the naked—some thought it a little too naked—story of a group of soldiers who take over a dug-out under which the Germans can be heard laying a mine. Plumer's historic blow-up at Messines, the fruit of long months of preparation and an instance of how a secret can be kept, came as a hideous surprise to the enemy ; suspense suggested with grim detail, the long-drawn-out waiting for something horrible that was sure to happen, though only God and some Germans knew when. There is scarcely any situation which does not lend itself to the soldier's jest and the author did much to colour, perhaps a little to dissipate, the dramatic tension through two acts with an unceasing supply of songs, jokes and war-time back-chat. But the tapping, tapping, went on through it all until with the beginning of the third act came the relieving party ; another section of infantry would be the victims ; the suspense of the men who had held the present trenches through long days and nights was over.

The play had been a little uneven in quality, but was crowned by a superb last five minutes in which Mr. Reginald Denham's skilful hand as a producer could be traced. The section of soldiers congratulating themselves on their relief is moving back over the duckboards. The men are halted and fallen out to rest ; some sleep the sleep of exhaustion, some prattle on under their breath. There is a sudden outbreak of shelling ; the mine has gone up under the trenches the men have just left, the enemy has broken through and the weary warriors who are out for a week's rest are ordered to reform and counter-attack. They move forward through a mist ; two fall, the others melt away in obscurity and confusion. There had been enacted one of those minor tragedies of the World War which the chronicler had almost to pass over, but which the historian has done something to emphasize.

There's a stir of youth in the Old House,
Whence the young life went West ;
The new life in the red fields
Is lying with riven breast,
But its Spirit comes to the Old House :
Abroad it cannot rest.

There are quick feet on the creaking stairs :
The lilt of a laughing song
Lightens the gloom of the Old House,
And heals a bitter wrong. . . .
From Fields of War to Homes of Love
Short space when nights are long.

There are eager eyes in the Old House
That seek their own again ;
Fingers that wake the lids of sleep
To dreams that are not in vain.
The Son returns to the Old House,
Though he sleeps among the slain.

" I do not remember in all my experience as a playgoer
having been kept awake by a play ; but last night I saw
Journey's End given by the Stage Society, and I could not
sleep for hours ; all day long I have been asking myself
the reason why. *Journey's End* is a thing by itself ;
suffering and death are about, but fun and laughter
often prevail. Of story there is little, of love interest
less ; thirty-six hours in a dug-out, the characters quite
ordinary soldiers—most of them ' for-the-period ' soldiers
—no picturesque exhibition either of German hate or
English heroism, no very thrilling event on the stage
except the death of the lately joined boy at the end, so
beautifully enacted that it was almost robbed of its
sadness, though it gave the final tug to one's heartstrings.

" Yet the writer—a simple, kindly fellow whose name
is hitherto unknown to anyone—has managed to convey
an idea, to represent an episode, with a force and a
fidelity for which in modern drama I do not easily find a
parallel. Drama, I believe, means action, and *Journey's*

End is action throughout; a progress with almost mechanical precision from cause to effect, but a progress so entirely human that all sense of theatre is absent.

" There will be some to say that the reality of the play may make it intolerable to those—like myself—whose hearts were torn from their breasts by the War ; others may think it undesirable to represent a British officer either as a coward or as something dangerously near a drunkard. Probably both these characters were true— perhaps rarely true—to type, because the one man was finally to overcome a weakness to which anyone might be prone, and the other, despite his addiction to the whiskey bottle, remains the resolute and adored leader of his men. And I think that those of us who mourn our ' unreturning brave ' will get crumbs of comfort from the reminder that despite all the squalor and the dirt, the blood and agony, there was good humour and good comradeship throughout, and that the joy of life was not wholly quenched even in the firing-line ; as one has seen for oneself, comedy and tragedy are closely interlaced in war, and mirth mocks at the heels of misery. The author was, I believe, all through those black weeks of 1918 ; he knows what he is writing about, and in some almost uncanny way he hangs before us the truest and the most haunting picture of the War that is likely to be made.

" Olivier, an ex-choirboy of All Saints', Margaret Street, plays the lead, but there is really no lead, as each character stands out like a cameo, yet each fits with equal value into the simplest and most suitable frame."

So runs a letter written on the morrow of seeing a play which was to make Europe and the overseas

Dominions hum with excitement and was to establish itself as the war play *par excellence* for all time.

Not the least remarkable performance of *Journey's End* was given by the Dramatic Society of the Royal Horse Guards ; an officer played the part of the coward, and as the rehearsals were strenuous, he was knocked down every evening for a month by a Corporal of Horse, who the next morning would gravely salute his superior at the stable doors. In no army in the world, as Marshal Foch himself said, when told about our system of Regimental sports, could this sort of thing be done without the slightest subversion of military discipline or etiquette.

There were some to murmur that the author's own proximity to the War had blurred his vision and that the characters he drew were not true to type. The answer was clean cut. Robert Sherriff would be the first to admit that the overwhelming majority of officers whether regulars or " for the duration," were no less temperate than brave ; he gave us two cases in which these virtues were not absent but seemed to hang in the balance. Stanhope drank, not to satisfy a lust but to stimulate nerves strained to snapping-point ; he would have met his death in those trenches in face of his country's enemy as brave and true and tender-hearted a soldier as ever drew sword. To no one but Stanhope was Hibbert's weakness really known, a weakness on which those who have never suffered from it should

CHAPTER XVIII

THE ACTOR-MANAGER

CRITICISM is never more beside the mark than when it condemns a system because of its incidental imperfections. Rather more than a little unfair has been the condemnation of what is nowadays referred to as " the good old " actor-manager régime which flourished before, and faded during, the War. Had it been superseded by a playwright-manager system, or better still by a millionaire-altruist-archangel-manager system, there might have been no pang of regret for its disappearance. But the miracle did not happen. To-day we are confronted with the commercial-manager who generally stands for a syndicate of business men ; as business men they have both eyes on the box-office, whereas the actor-manager anyhow used one eye for the discovery of plays which (at worst) would pander to his vanity as an actor and (at best) would quite justly combine this with his prestige as a manager.

The fly in the ointment of the actor-manager system was that plays were chosen because the leading part was one in which the man in authority would shine conspicuously ; this was not altogether to be deprecated because, as a matter of fact, most plays which are a good commercial proposition, contain a " fat " part, and with men of sterling merit and varied gifts, such as Irving, Tree, Alexander, Wyndham—to quote the leading lights —the fat part would swell even larger in its performance. The real misfortune was that dramatists, instead of giving free rein to their pens, were tempted to contrive plays specially adapted for the liking of the prospective purchaser ; there was also the tendency to create three, or four, stereotyped acts in which the same characters, with their environment, having once asserted themselves, were trotted out again and again in so-called " new and original comedies." A stereotyped hero of a particular brand of play was one we should now be disposed to call an unmitigated prig. He stood out in *The Walls of Jericho* and other, more or less, contemporary Society dramas ; his *raison d'être* was the chastisement of smart Society. To emphasize his difference from the worthless people around him, and at the same time explain his presence among them, he was generally one of those at that time popular characters, the " Men from the Colonies," or perhaps from America, some place anyway where " men were men," and where " roughing it " could be luckily combined with the accumulation of a fortune. The cash was a passport into Society where the he-man showed his simple faith in human nature by immediately marrying the daughter of an impoverished

Just now also the playwright was busy with the sharp reaction against the growing emancipation of women. How few of us remain to remember Winifred Emery's captivating *New Woman*, whose domestic redemption was sealed with a promise to " love honour *and obey*." The women were either so intensely feminine as to be rather silly and helpless, or they were depicted as so abusing their freedom as to be led by it into some tight corner from which the ultra-manly man had to rescue them. Not until the War, when women were called on, and sprang, to perform every sort of duty for which men had hitherto been regarded as indispensable, did the real emancipation of the sex stamp itself both on real life and the drama.

The actor-manager—and here lurked another danger— had of course two distinct, and sometimes mutually antagonistic, interests to bear in mind. Where his honourable ambition as an artist said " Yes " to a manuscript which he had eagerly read, the box-office would interpose with a stern " No." Macaulay said of Pitt and Grenville that the one saw nothing but the glory and the other nothing but the bills ! Irving and Tree were decidedly on Pitt's side, Tree going so far as to be impatient of a " run " because it prevented his making a fresh start. Kendal solved the difficulty by attending to the business side himself, leaving his talented wife, subject to his advice, to direct the stage. Something approaching the converse of the Kendal system was believed to obtain at the Criterion. George Alexander studied the question from both angles, and was not at all averse to risking on the roundabouts of Art some of the profits he derived from the swings of more commercial plays. That splendid veteran, Sir John Martin-Harvey, has been ready to pay out over his Covent Garden *Hamlet* a large lump of the profits he derived from touring England in *The Only Way* and other old plays of the same kidney which, anyhow until lately, provincial audiences seem to assimilate with insatiable appetite.

No actor-manager, not even Irving himself, pretended that he was out for Art and nothing else ; even apart from the matter of pure finance, drama fades in importance if it does not attract a paying, as distinct from a paper, public ; the treasury could not be disregarded, however alluring the call of glory. But at present it would almost seem as if the other side were upwards. The ordinary commercial-manager or impersonal syndicate places financial reward above all others, however aware that the public generally identifies the play it likes with the actors or possibly the author and is very languidly interested in the management responsible for putting the play on. A striking exception, of course, is Mr. C. B. Cochran. By a persistent policy of self-advertisement comparable with that of Bernard Shaw in the realm of authorship— and beside which Mr. Selfridge in the region of commerce pales altogether—Mr. Cochran has so completely identified his productions with himself that " a Cochran

he submitted it was a personal friend. For two whole months the post brought him no news. It then happened that a rival manager, hearing by chance of the existence of this play, wrote and asked for a copy. The author, not having one by him, wrote to the first manager and asked for an immediate return of his manuscript, to receive an alarmed request that it might be retained for a further twenty-four hours to give this functionary an opportunity of reading it. If a comedy by a fairly well-known writer can repose in a drawer for two months only to be taken out through the provocation of a rival's interest, one wonders what must be the fate of many plays by unknown authors.

CHAPTER XIX

CHARLES HAWTREY

Not surely so long since we saw him,
Health brimming in feature and limb.
Let me try to imagine and draw him
Ere fancy and feature are dim.
Dark, eager, a face to remember,
A flush that could change as the day,
A spirit that knew not December,
That brightened the spirit of May.

A PRIVATE school—kept by his kindly, but rather formidable, father—Eton, a brief and not very brilliant experience as owners of racehorses in the '80's, supper-parties protracted to unconscionable hours, meetings to organize charity performances, long talks in the dressing-room to which free access was given and from which was not excluded even the gentleman who " wanted his account settled," the War Office where, during the long struggle, he would come to ask, a little vaguely but quite sincerely, if he could be of any use ; these were some of the points of contact one had with Charlie Hawtrey, and with each and every one life always seemed to be just a shade more brightly coloured.

than the creditor to make a proposal. Hawtrey's aplomb was no stage trick but was ingrained in his character; one can scarcely think of anyone else who would succeed in getting in direct telephone touch with the Chancellor of the Exchequer and protest to that august official of the ruthlessness and unfairness with which he was pursued by the " taxes."

Now and again Hawtrey would be out of the bill ; then, however competent his understudy, one realized how much knowledge of, and care for, his art lay beneath the ease with which every point was scored. He never moved a finger (and his hands were as eloquent as his lips) without meaning, and conveying, something ; the infinite pains which he took over a particular phrase often went far to illumine a whole play When he seemed laziest he might be working his hardest, when he seemed crassly stupid he was using all his wits to give the effect of a slow brain ; when he was apparently strolling through his part, every nerve might really be strung and his body bathed in perspiration.

His popularity may have sought to spoil him but certainly never succeeded in doing so. He was in request everywhere, not so much for what he was willing to do, but for what he was. Did the Duchess of Devonshire want theatricals got up at Chatsworth to amuse King Edward ; Charles Hawtrey would come down and not only coach the distinguished amateurs but take his part with them. The result was a little uneven, but that only made it the better fun. Did Lady Ripon think Queen Alexandra and the Empress Marie would like a little comedy or duologue played after an *intime* Sunday dinner at Coombe ; Hawtrey could be relied on to find the exact actress to play with, and up to, him ; and the Royal ladies would have a delicate little dramatic feast set out for them. Was a hospital in dire need of funds ; Hawtrey would organize a matinée, and so long as the main object was secure, would care little whether he got anything like his full share of credit for it. Was a friend, or dependent, on the rocks ? Well, according to the old adage that only the poor help the poor, help would somehow be scraped up. Finance was never his forte, and lack of funds may at times have led him into errors of judgment : but they were errors of the head and not of the heart and they were frankly owned and fully atoned for. As an actor Hawtrey had his limitations and knew them ; as a *bon enfant* he had none. May the earth lie light on the ashes of one of the best of " good companions."

tain, hideous threats of tearing his —— entrails from his —— body were hurled at him.

Realism, no less ambitious, has now swung to the other extreme, and may tend to resolve itself into precluding whatever savours of stage effect in delivery of spoken word or appropriate gesture.

Farce and melodrama are privileged eccentrics and in the Realism of interest just now lies the approximation to so-called natural acting which is aimed at in comedy and comedy drama. If it is true that all plays must be realistic in the one sense, it is equally true that a really realistic play, with really realistic dialogue as applied to-day, would empty Drury Lane as quickly as a cry of Fire would empty the tiny Duchess Theatre. Few people realize what their own, or other people's, conversation is like, how ungrammatical, often almost to the point of unintelligibility, how rambling and inconsequential, how untidy ; the art of the playwright consists largely in (to borrow a word from Hollywood) "grooming" conversation into dialogue; it is the paradoxical art of translating something genuine into something wholly artificial which nevertheless will fall on the ears of the audience as even more genuine than the real thing, if spoken, would seem.

"The 'istory of 'Arrow," said a janitor of that school to a group of visitors, "is an 'istory of 'itches." Something of the same sort might apply to the story of dramatic writing as it unfolds a gradual and, at times, rather painful approach to verisimilitude. It is not unlikely that over and over again the dramatic author has turn sheets of his manuscript in two, the producer has reconsidered his directions *da capo*, because they felt that there was something a little out-of-date about their efforts. It all seemed so straightforward when they started, but the difficulty of adjusting plot and production to present-day outlook was a difficulty which pulled them up with an awkward jerk at many a corner. To compare the dialogue of a Pinero, or an early Somerset Maugham, play with the conversation of a Noel Coward comedy is to appreciate how sharp a change has occurred even within the experience of the comparatively young. But dialogue, however modern, however rapid and even clipped, however punctuated with puffs of cigarette smoke, is still apt to have the flavour of artificiality of which few artists, other than M. Lucien Guitry, have been able wholly to strip it.

As with dialogue, so with acting ; the reproach used to be levelled at that incomparable modern actor, Gerald Du Maurier, that he didn't " act " ; he merely " behaved," he was merely himself. Never was criticism wider of the truth ; Gerald Du Maurier was, from the crown of his head to the sole of his foot, one of the most " theatrical " actors of his day. He did not, as so many people, cheaply, commented, " walk through " his parts ; rather would he, with consummate art, get an intensely dramatic effect while deluding the audience into regarding as a quite casual natural movement a

demonstrativeness due to racial characteristics with acting as an art. Max Beerbohm in one of his Essays describes Frenchmen drinking their aperitifs outside the Café de la Paix as all " excited in conversation about something or other." A casual observer would have thought some national or private crisis was the subject matter of these conversations. But no ! one group was " differing as to the age of a well-known Spanish dancer ; the two men on my left are agreeing as to the merits of a new kind of automobile ; in front of me two other men are deciding where they shall have breakfast. . . . They talked with their hands, with all the muscles of their faces, with all the resources of their lungs, with their whole souls and bodies. . . . The Englishman, *per contra*, is averse from any expressiveness. When he breaks silence, he breaks it in a mumble or a monotone. His face is a mask. His body is a log. His hands are useless except for manual labour. Inflect or gesticulate he cannot." With natural acting such as is seen on the boulevards, is it any surprise that the French are better equipped for the stage than the British ; it is largely a question of temperament. When we use the word " theatrical " we imply the very opposite of natural and suggest a regrettable failure on the part of someone to preserve the restraint and reticence on which we pride ourselves. Violent emotion is, or is said to be, essentially un-English, and by dubbing such a display as theatrical we associate the theatre with a demonstrativeness which in

(Photo by Yvonne Gregory)

JOHN GIELGUD

[Facing p. 222

than art. And that "something" is precisely w at the public means and understands by Acting. Not ra. ting; not just reckless histrionic fireworks; but something which, while it need never for a moment "o'erstep the modesty of nature," dramatizes, rather than exactly mirrors, the body, mind and spirit of mankind. And that "something" may have a good deal to do with the future of the British Theatre.

And if a label is required for it, what about National Romanticism?

CHAPTER XXI

ABOUT SOME CRITICS

CRITICISM, we are officially reminded, is the action of passing judgment on the qualities or merits of anything, especially the passing of unfavourable judgment. Authors and artists, who have winced with pain or trembled with anger under notices either hostile or damning with faint praise, would perhaps say that the men of letters who to-day form the corps of dramatic critics are too prone to the " unfavourable " ; they might think that, anyhow as regards the theatre, Bishop Dowden was scarcely justified in writing more than half a century ago, " that the effort of criticism in our time has been to see things as they are without partiality, without obtrusion of personal liking or disliking." The good Bishop was anyhow nearer the mark even in his time than the satirist who some years earlier, when dramatic criticism had admittedly sunk very low, wrote with vinegared pen : " Poor things, they've got their little weaknesses, no doubt. They're apt to sit out first performances at the refreshment-bar or nearest ' pub,' where they'll ask, ' How's it going ? ' and record a

225   P

" trash " still flourished. Ibsen, of course, was the new great idol ; but what about Pinero ? Was he the real thing or merely a clever faker ? Here the New School critics were sharply divided. Genius was a word which must be used with all reserve, but Archer maintained that anybody who denied Pinero's genius must be " the victim of a paralysing prejudice."

" All I can say is," retorted Max Beerbohm, " that if Mr. Archer is right, mine is a clear case of paralysis. . . . I never saw or read a play of Pinero's without admiring his skill ; but genius I never scented there." Max Beerbohm was reinforced by Bernard Shaw, who thought that Pinero attracted the public

" by the exquisite flattery of giving them plays which they really liked, whilst persuading them that such appreciation was only possible from persons of great culture and intellectual acuteness."

For three short years, from 1895 to 1898, Bernard Shaw, as one of a brilliant all-round staff, was responsible to the " Saturday Review " for dramatic criticism ; what he and his distinguished followers, Mr. James Agate and Mr. Ivor Brown, did and dared, gave to the " Saturday Review " among the " weeklies " the same outstanding theatrical importance which the " Telegraph " enjoyed among the " dailies." However sharply Bernard Shaw and Clement Scott differed in tastes, in method, in outlook, they had in common a genuine love for the theatre and a no less genuine desire to impart this passion to their readers. They were serious but never, like Archer or Grein, solemn ; neither of them would have spoken, as Grein did, of holding " the office of dramatic criticism as sacred as the exalted functions of Her Majesty's Judges." Solemnity has been described as seriousness without a sense of humour. Laughter in Court—except when it is sycophancy to the Judge—is a far worse thing than laughter in Church. And, anyhow within the pages of the " Saturday Review," Shaw's constant laughter was a constant source of strength. It made his criticisms wholly readable by other people besides the Ibsenites and did much to persuade those who were hanging back that the drama of Ideas could scarcely be dull. And what a mine of wit is to be quarried in those two volumes of Dramatic Opinions, and how astute was their writer when he begged his readers " not to mistake my journalistic utterances for final estimates." If only the modern biographers would lay these words to heart ! How often in the volumes dealing with the great figures of the Great War words dropped by men—and especially by soldiers—under the pressure of great excitement or sudden emergency, have, with cruel unfairness, been recorded as if they were settled opinions.

To follow Bernard Shaw was appointed a man of very different stamp, and perhaps was offered to the readers of the " Saturday " as a well-earned holiday after three strenuous years in Mr. Shaw's Academy of Learning.

But if he was a holiday-tutor, there was no intention that the holiday should be a period of intellectual idleness. Max was as much an All-for-Ibsen-and-the-World-Well-Loster as his predecessor. It was simply that the lessons were less formally didactic, and the birch was at least not a visible threat.

He approached his task with misgivings and without enthusiasm. His very first essay is significantly entitled: " Why I Ought Not to have Become a Dramatic Critic." And when he went on to explain : " I am not a person of expensive habits, but I confess that I have never regarded any theatre as much more than the conclusion to a dinner or the prelude to a supper," those who were used to Shaw's self-confidence and dogmatic statements must have wondered whether this appointment was not either a profound mistake or a rather sorry joke.

Shaw, when bidding good-bye to his readers, referred to his successor as " the incomparable Max." His readers' queries as to " Incomparably what ? " were answered a week after Max " took over " when Coquelin —whom Sarah once described as " not a great artist but the greatest actor alive "—brought *Cyrano* to London. The critics were unanimous as to Coquelin being a great actor, but they were not quite so sure whether *Cyrano* was a great classic. Max Beerbohm's contribution to the controversy was characteristic if not incomparable. " It is," he wrote with entire confidence, " at least a wonderfully ingenious counterfeit of a classic likely to

deceive experts far more knowing than I am." Then
Rostand had declared that Cyrano's very soul had passed
into the actor who impersonated him. Max was not
quite sure.

" Some of it—the comic, which is, perhaps, the greater
part of it—has done so. But I am afraid that the tragic
part is still floating somewhere, unembodied. Perhaps
the two parts will never be embodied together in the
same actor."

How far Cyrano had projected himself into the soul
of Coquelin may be gauged by the total inability of
Charles Wyndham even to suggest the soldier of Gascony
when Rostand's masterpiéce was unhappily put on at
the Criterion in 1900. There were some of us to feel
that one compensation for being engaged in the dreary
Boer warfare was that we were precluded from witnessing
the failure of one of the most brilliant and polished
comedians whom the English stage has known when
attacking a part wholly unsuited to him.

The London theatre was just now humming with
excitement. Bernard Shaw's earlier plays were being
discussed by excited groups ; Pinero was still a subject
for controversy ; Henry Arthur Jones [1] was not being

[1] Henry Arthur Jones confided to the present writer that he regarded Sardou not as a great dramatic writer but as a supremely
clever dramatic carpenter. "It is very interesting to know what
Henry Arthur Jones thinks of Sardou," murmured W. S. Gilbert
when the remark was repeated to him. "It would be even more
interesting to know what Sardou thinks of Henry Arthur Jones."

undervalued ; Barrie was dawning on the London public. In June 1899 Sarah arrived at the Adelphi to play Hamlet. Max Beerbohm was always one of Sarah's staunchest champions. "Pre-eminently great throughout the past four decades," he wrote of her, and stinging was his contempt for the rival Duseites whose voices are "uplifted in unisonant dithyrambus."

"Night after night the English public sits solemnly at the Lyceum (having paid higher prices than it pays for a play in its own language), tremendously bored, tremendously edified. . . . If a fiery chariot were seen waiting outside the stage-door, no one would be much surprised."

How many people were as honest as he was to confess their inability to compare Sarah with Duse because, with a fair working knowledge of French, they were entirely ignorant of the Italian language ? As to technique, and of Elena's technique there could be no doubt, "technique," writes her arch-critic, "is a nice relation of the mime's voice, gesture and facial expression to the words by him or her spoken"; and if these words are "so much gibberish, how can you pass any judgment on the mime's technique?"

There was a second way of "raving" about the Duse who, curiously enough, drew rather "skinny" houses when she was at the heyday of her career, while she played to capacity when she was evidently a tired woman. This was in regard to her conception of a part, as to which anyone who had read the play might justifiably form an opinion. Max Beerbohm declared that he knew the rôles of Magda, Paula Tanqueray, Fédora and the Princesse Georges " well enough to be convinced that Duse has no conception of any one of them." He admired her grace and could not but admire her exquisite and eloquent hands ; he saw power and nobility in her face and thought her admirable in *La Gioconda* which happened to suit her, but his prevailing impression was " of a great egoistic force, of a woman over-riding with an air of sombre unconcern plays, mimes, critics, and public," and, " in the name of Art," he protested against it.

Sarah was Max Beerbohm's idol, Sarah with her volcanic nature and not less volcanic career. He dubs her " the greatest of living tragediennes " and lingers over her " genius that has so often thrilled me beyond measure." And when her memoirs were published and he sat reading them in a little village on the coast of Italy, he felt like " a somnambulist awaking to find himself peering into the crater of a volcano." In the same rapturous terms he writes of Sarah's chisel and her brush ; these rhapsodies may have been induced in some degree by the warmth of an Italian sun, for, as a matter of fact, Sarah's book had little literary merit, and she admittedly learnt sculpture and painting far less for themselves than because the lessons were of great value to her own Art. The practice with pencil and brush prompted many a decision as to *mise en scène*, while assuredly the knowledge of sculpture, however superficial, could be reckoned with in emphasizing the actress's power to convey a world of meaning, not only with movement of head and hands, but with every turn and twist of her sinuous body.

Long may Mr. James Agate lead his readers, Sunday by Sunday, along the flowered bypaths, which he deliciously opens to them, but more than one generation may pass before A. B. Walkley is dethroned from the position in which " The Times " newspaper so wisely placed, and as long as possible retained, him. A little addicted to the quotation of French novelists, and a little too apt, for the unscholarly, to cite the dramatic laws of Aristotle, his work was scholarly and gentle, void of anything that might offend, and as such carrying on the traditions of the great newspaper. When Mr. Delane—whose kindly hospitality is a pleasant personal souvenir—was the great editor, his dramatic critic, John Oxenford, had penned a criticism, as a result of which an indignant actor had written to the editor in violent protest. Delane sent for his critic and reproved him with the words : " These things don't interest the general public. So look here, my dear fellow, write me accounts of plays henceforth that won't bring me any more such letters."

The dramatic criticism of to-day in this country is kindly in intent and as such not as exciting as the "wise-cracking" notices on which New York gloats. The trouble is that some editors seem to hug themselves with the idea that their readers are no longer interested in the theatre. Whether or no it be true that some newspaper proprietors have large financial interests in the Cinema, it is anyhow certain that while whole pages are devoted by the more popular journals to the Pictures, a brief paragraph is often sufficient to report a first night in the playhouse. Even in the more serious papers the space devoted to dramatic criticism is shrinking with each passing year, and Mr. Darlington might well complain, as some of us do, that he only enjoys less than a fifth of the space allotted to Clement Scott who filled a column and a half of closely printed type with his first-night notices.

And Scott had till one in the morning for his writing. With our modern hustle and keen competition between newspapers, only Mr. Morgan of "The Times" has anything approaching leisure. "Normally," one well-known critic tells me, "I can reckon on forty-five minutes." But special circumstances may curtail this— a long play, for instance, or one which starts, and therefore ends, late. "Practically speaking, I *must* be finished by midnight." As for the space allotted to his notice, he regards about one-third of a column as the normal length. But he adds a significant, imaginary dialogue by way of illustration, which ends thus :

Night Editor : How much space do you want ?
Critic : As much as I can get.
Night Editor : Well,. keep it as short as you can, or you'll be cut. There's no room at all to-night.

Curiously enough, the critics do not as a whole complain of the shortness of the time in which they have to accomplish an often difficult task. Some maintain that the hurry acts as a spur, and others are wholly doubtful whether another hour devoted to the criticism would make it any better ; the lightning sketch can be quite as true as the laboriously finished study in oils.

In fine, the layman is forced to the conclusion that if the critic's duty seems one of equal difficulty and delicacy, the critics themselves enjoy the chains in which they labour and are not dissatisfied with the results ; it is even possible to think that disappointed playwrights, managers and artists would be a little happier if they realized the difficult conditions under which their judges have to work.

CHAPTER XXII

THE THEATRE AND THE CINEMA

TIME and again the Theatre finds itself " up against " some new and, at first sight, serious difficulty. Even the vogue of the popular novel moved certain dreary prophets to shake their heads ominously as to the blow which might well fall on the comparatively few theatres then existing. The advent of the Movies was sadly, but confidently, expected to have much the same effect on the theatre as the entrance of poverty pro- verbially exercises on love. The post-war epidemic of dancing, when even the schoolboy, who had already given the pantomime the go-by, admitted his preference for the parquet over the play, could not but give to many playhouses cause for real anxiety. Daylight-saving and the consequent new opportunities for outdoor evening games sounded yet another death-knell for the Theatre, and when the Movies became the Talkies many people simply shrugged their shoulders with the surmise that the time was at hand when theatres would either close their doors or convert themselves into super- cinemas.

And yet in this year of grace 1935, on more than one stifling evening in the midst of a July heat-wave, people were turned away from a theatre in Shaftesbury Avenue where a well-acted play of no outstanding merit was being performed for about the hundredth time ; the house was brim full from floor to ceiling.

Very peculiar are the fortunes of the Theatre. For no apparent reason, at one moment very poor houses have to be recorded, a month later " House Full " boards have to be propped up outside almost every West End playhouse. How to understand the public's rapidly alternating moods of eagerness and indifference ? The fat times are never quite satisfactorily accounted for even by the urbane officials at the theatrical libraries ; for the lean times there is never any lack of what Americans call " alibis." Hot weather, cold weather, fine weather, wet weather—these may all be glibly quoted to explain a week of empty houses.

If an outsider might suggest one reason for the fluctuating interest in the drama, it would be that the public has a very sensitive theatrical pulse, and that a series of five or six rather flat productions induces the reflection that to book seats at a theatre is a rather poor way of spending money. Some other attraction crops up, the theatrical column in the daily papers is languidly perused, if at all, and, especially in the long summer days, not even the well-tested and really good plays can attract large audiences. Then suddenly some piece is put on and,

238

whether its notices be good or bad, catches the attention of the public. "I want to see that," people begin to say. And they ring up for seats, or queue up in the street outside the pit and many of them find they can't get in, and drift away to try some other neighbouring theatre. And those who do get in and enjoy the play, and those who are unable to get in that night but are quite determined to try again some other night, all with one consent begin to talk about that play, and then about other plays, and the Theatre gets back into "from day-to-day" conversation. Or to use an Americanism, the public becomes "theatre-conscious." And then begins one of the sunny waves of prosperity.

A tough Die-hard has been the notion that the so-called Season is the time in which the theatres largely flourish ; only with difficulty, and after suffering considerable pecuniary loss, have foreign companies and artists been persuaded that the converse is the fact. When the days are long and Ascot, Lord's, the river, Wimbledon, have paramount claims and preclude the dislocation of a day for early dinner, the theatres are naturally liable to wilt. More than one playwright has been heard to say that the best moment to produce a new play is the end of July when special appeal is made to visitors in hotels from the provinces and abroad whose evenings are disengaged. If the play has any merit at all it gets well aired and may have settled down into a steady success before the Londoners return from holiday-making.

That the Talkies are a dangerous rival to the Theatres is a commonplace. Admittedly they are cheap and they are comfortable, and to millions of people they are not only luxurious but decoratively " very handsome." And above all, they are, for the millions, convenient. Except in very remote country places few people in England need look further than a motor coach or motor omnibus to land them in a picture palace ; no great time is spent in the traject and a tidy sum of money is saved which the Theatre would have swallowed up. To those endowed with this world's goods, who do not shrink from a seat at eight and sixpence, the saving of four shillings may not be a very strong inducement, but even for these it means something that they need not alter their dinner hour or hurry away dyspeptically from a " bolted " meal ; the lazy need not go through the exertion of putting on evening dress, the slovenly need not even change their flannel shirts ; only in exceptional circumstances need seats be booked beforehand ; as late as nine o'clock the sudden decision can be registered to " go to something," and it means a good deal to be able to do so. The Cinema, too, caters for all tastes ; many of the more " sophisticated " patrons of the Cinema prefer the shorter, less pretentious " Silly Symphonies," the News-reels, and the Travel or other so-called " educational " films, to the " All-Star-Super-Laugh-Thrill " or whatever the current " masterpiece " may be. Lastly, the Cinema's irresistible claim is the

impossibility of being bored by every item on its programme. And even if bored, boredom is less acute
because in the darkness the individual can relax mentally
as well as physically. Truly the Talkies are blown
forward by favourable winds !

And there are other, less direct, influences at work to
stiffen them in their fight against the Theatre ; publicity,
with all its sensationalism and its stunts, and the mob-
hysteria provoked by what Hollywood frankly and
cynically calls " dope." The popular newspaper runs
some risks if it does not give half a dozen items of so-
called " news " relating to so-called " film stars."
Nor is it only Hollywood's large financial resources and
larger commercial enterprise which enables it to crowd
the daily and weekly journals with paragraphs and
photographs and to render the Press a magnificent shop-
window for the Pictures. There is something else—
something so entirely alien to English character that the
English Theatre can have no sort of retaliation. Hollywood film world does not claim more than a bowing
acquaintance with decency. Perish the thought that an
English actress would consent, in order to boost her play
or swell her salary, to have lying rumours run their
course about her private life. But there is scarcely a day
in the life of a Hollywood film star on which she is not
" rumoured " to be suing for a divorce or contemplating
marriage—licensed concubinage would be the more
appropriate term—with a male star of flashy or beefy

appearance and dubious habits, or better still with a nebulous Balkan Prince, an English Peer, or an American " king." Then comes the denial of the rumour ; more subtly still the refusal to admit it. Spice the meaningless denial of a manufactured rumour, pay generously for its circulation, and the world is ready to receive the stars " latest and greatest " Masterpiece of Motion-Picture Drama ! How can a self-respecting English actress score against the film star who " denies the rumour " that she has been secretly married to the Crown Prince of Esperanto ?

Again there is the lure of the fantastic salaries offered by the Films—even by the soi-disant " British " Films— to youthful and quite inexperienced stage-players, especially young girls. So soon as she has shown some signs of knowing her business, a young actress is lured away. Why, she asks, should she not exchange a few years of experience in minor rôles at a salary not exceeding £20 per week, for the Films when these are dangling stardom coupled with more than ten times that sum in front of her ? Besides, to refuse is to run the risk of " missing the boat " ; she knows perfectly well that it is her youth, with its attendant inexperience, for which the Films are willing to pay.

Nor are the British " Hollywoods " so far from Shaftesbury Avenue that a nimble actress cannot live a double life, a Stage and Screen life. Her marriage to the Stage still exists while a liaison is contracted with the Talkies.

She postpones the making absolute the *decree nisi*—the "nisi," of course, being a pecuniary proviso. The alliance will continue to subsist *unless* the theatrical manager, blind to the new "revaluation of all values," refuses to pay the inexperienced small-part actress a salary at least three times as great as she, or the part she is to play, is worth. Here is the second of the injuries inflicted by the squander-mania of the Talkies. First the young actresses desert the ship; then they consent to return—at an admiral's rate of pay!

Evidently then, in respect of cheapness, comfort, convenience for the audience, the salaries offered to artists and the guaranteed security of earnings flourished before writers, the Cinemas have got the Theatres "whacked." That is the truth, but happily not the whole truth, or the future of London Theatres would be a sorry one.

What is the factor which, despite all the increased technical perfection of the Cinema, despite the coming of colour, and stereoscopy, will preserve the Theatre as a living and, with all its ups and downs, a thriving Art? The only answer is that the Cinema, whatever point of perfection it may reach, can only be a photograph, a reproduction, a second-hand, and (as it were) an unreal thing. When a film is good—and how very good many of them are—the audience may not be conscious of the purely photo-phonographic nature of the entertainment. But they are quite possibly subconscious of it; some

243

part of their mental or emotional appetite is being neglected. May one say that the Cinema is lacking in " Vitamin X," the " X " here representing something mysterious but withal stimulating, and anyhow essential to full and complete enjoyment of an acted play. Is it to trespass into pure speculation to suppose that in the Cinema one is subconsciously aware that the drama on the screen is not contemporaneous ; that it is not at this moment being enacted before us but has already been enacted in the past and what we see is but a diabolically clever reconstruction of it ? Is it not true that this part of illusion, the very essence of theatrical enjoyment, tricks us all willingly into believing in the Theatre that the future really is the future, and that what is to come in the story is not already fixed. Truly it is not always fixed, for one may cite as an episode in the history of those splendid Canterbury players. Many years ago one of the star amateur actors was cast to play a butler, one of those innocuous servants who are little more than human " properties." The actor looked at his part, his face became as long as a fiddle-string, for he had only a commonplace menial line to say in each of the three acts. But he made no comment, uttered no disgruntled protest ; he rehearsed his part with due humility and waited for the " night." Halfway through Act One, prompt on his cue, the butler entered and informed Her Ladyship that the carriage was ready, and Her Ladyship said, " Thank you,

Jenkins." And then, instead of the " Exit Jenkins" which the script directed, Jenkins, with complete composure, startled Her Ladyship by giving notice ! There was nothing for it but to carry on as though his unpremeditated scene were part of the play, and Her Ladyship (inspired, no doubt, by similar domestic thunderbolts in her private life) asked " Why ? " Whereupon, with the fluency of long rehearsal, Jenkins launched forth into an eloquent statement of his many pent-up grievances : the inconsiderateness of his mistress, the insufficiency and poor quality of the food provided for the upper servants, the inferior nature of His Lordship's cigars [1]—et cetera. It was a long and brilliant monologue, and he ended by informing his embarrassed mistress that he was leaving the house at once.

But " the future " in his case held something more in store than this new episode. Unknown to anyone except the actor, there was to be a new character. For Jenkins had some more of those dull menial lines to say in Act

---

[1] An analogous incident occurred in real life to the writer's knowledge, in the country house of an Evangelical Baronet where Thornton's Family Prayers were in daily use. The master of the house thought that extemporary orisons would make an agreeable change and invited contributions from the household. So long as only the butler and the housekeeper voiced the aspirations of their fellows, all went well ; but one fine morning an insubordinate kitchenmaid chipped in with : " And we pray for Sir Thomas and Her Ladyship too. Oh, may they have new hearts given to them ! " The bare thought that there was room for such renovation caused a prompt and permanent return to Henry Thornton.

Two ; and Jenkins had not repented of the " notice " he had given. Jenkins was gone, for good. When his cue came in the second act, instead of Jenkins, there appeared an old, old butler, with long white hair and long white whiskers. And before anybody on the stage had time to recover from their amazement, this venerable old gentleman was telling them that he was Jenkins' father, who had come to take his son's place ; and from this he proceeded to relate his own career, and how in his time he had been at one time footman to Lord This, and then butler to Lord That. And then, at the very end, he spoke the single wretched little line the author had provided, and the play continued. . . .

Now, of course, such unpremeditated scenes are very infrequent in the Theatre, though even in straight plays actors have been known to introduce a line without warning ; Beerbohm Tree and Gerald Du Maurier would take impish amusement in thus embarrassing their colleagues. But the point is that night after night an audience will sit through a play entirely possessed by the illusion that the drama they are witnessing is a real and contemporaneous occurrence, and this because the Stage —unlike the Cinema—does *really* re-enact anew that drama every time. This suggestion may be entirely lame and inadequate, but some explanation there must be to account for the triumphant survival of the Drama, and for the fact that the Cinema—despite all it can offer in comfort, cheapness and convenience, despite its

246

boundless financial resources, despite methods of sales-
manship with which the Stage would disdain to compete
—has failed to crush or to deal even a really effective
blow to the Theatre.

With Sarah Bernhardt—the greatest artist whom three
generations have looked on—the book should have
begun ; with Sarah anyhow it shall end.

" The Theatre is irresistible, organize it." Such was
her farewell advice to the British public than whom
advowedly she found no other so faithful. She would
speak of the fact that by a freak of circumstance one of
the few countries which feels the restraining hand of
the Censor is a country which enjoys no helping hand
from the State, that here the State has no concern for,
no interest in, the Theatre, however important in the
national life, however salutary for National manners.
But Sarah was a clear as well as a sympathetic visionary,
and she perhaps foresaw what, if she were among us,
she would see to-day ; a profession which has organized
itself in proud independence of any official sustenance ;
theatres which for comfort and dignity put to shame
almost any theatre in Europe ; plays—after due discount
allowed for rubbish which should be food for the waste-
paper basket—written not to show off this or that star
but calculated to be some contribution to dramatic

247

literature ; loyal team work, the precise opposite of Catalini's *Moi et quelques poupées*, repertory theatres where selfless, and often self-sacrificing, efforts are made towards building up reputations of authors and artistes alike ; audiences critical of what is bad and generously appreciative of what is good, and actors and actresses who seem more and more to remember that the greater the demand on them the more eager should be their response, who recognize that the players are there for the play and not the play for the players and who abundently realize that it is " my work " which should fill, as it adorns, their lives and above all who do not forget that to-day's work, whether marked by success or the reverse, is chiefly valuable as a preparation for the day's work to come.

INDEX

INDEX

Moliére, 53
Money, 41, 42, 44
Money Spinner, The, 89
Monte Cristo Junior, 123
Moody, Louise, 69
Moore, Eva, 162
Moore, Grace, 17
Moore, Mary, 81
Morand, Eugene, 179
Moses in Egypt, 29
Mottram, R. H., 189
Mounet, Paul, 161
M.P., 36
Mrs. Gorringe's Necklace, 205
Musical Comedy, 121 ff.
My Awful Dad, 213

Nares, Owen, 143
Nesbitt, Cathleen, 157
Nethersole, Olga, 51, 140
New Magdalen, 136
New Theatre, 109
New Women, 206
Nicholson, Watson, 28
Nielson, Adelaide, 106, 107
Nightingale, Florence, 128
Nos Intimes, 39, 49
Notorious Mrs. Ebbsmith, The, 129
Novello, Ivor, 174

Odds and Ends, 208
Odette, 70 f.
Old Vic, 157
Olivier, Laurence, 82, 110, 198
On Approval, 154
Only Way, The, 207
O'Regan, Kathleen, 156
Our Betters, 149, 153
Ours, 36, 40, 44
Overland Route, 41

Oxenford, John, 234

Palace of Truth, 88
Parker, Louis, 170
Partners, 48
Payne, Teddie, 125
Peg Woffington, 41, 72
Peril, 39, 49
Perrin, M., 53
Phèdre, 54 ff., 60
Phelps, Samuel, 17, 33, 114
Pierson, Blanche, 48, 169
Pinero, Sir A., 81, 89, 127, 130,
    135, 136 ff., 147, 152, 219,
    228, 231
Plumer, Viscount, 195
Prices, 39
Priestley, J. B., 130, 141, 159
Prince of Wales's Theatre, 37,
    39, 40, 42, 49
Princess and the Butterfly, The, 144
Prisoners of War, 192
Prisonnière, La, 141
Private Secretary, The, 212
Profligate, The, 135, 136

Quin, 23 f.

Rachel, 32, 56, 58, 183
Racine, 53, 60, 141
Raymond, Ernest, 189
Reade, Charles, 41
Realism, 216 ff.
Red Lamp, The, 134
Regan, General John, 213
Rehearsing, 172 ff.
Rehan, Ada, 114
Reichemberg, Mlle, 88
Réjane, Gabrielle, 46, 124
Rich, John, 24

INDEX